Prayers of Power

Prayers of Power

Coedited by:
Arthur Foote II
John F. Hayward
Kenneth Read-Brown
Bruce Southworth

Herbert F. Vetter,
General Editor

Harvard Square Library
www.harvardsquarelibrary.org

Designed by Andrew Drane

Prayers of Power

Published by Harvard Square Library
www.harvardsquarelibrary.org

ISBN: 978-0-6152-4407-5

Contents

Selections, by Author

Preface

Prayer is an act of making the world whole again. An anonymous person once put the issue in a single word:

> *Here is a prayer to be said*
> *when the world has gotten you down*
> *and you feel rotten,*
> *and you've got too much to do,*
> *and you're mad at everybody,*
> *and you're too tired to pray:*
> *HELP!*

Our frailties amidst the perplexities of life encourage us to look beyond our little selves to the larger Life enfolding and sustaining us, thereby making the world whole again.

Humanity East and West, in quest of health and wholeness, has created a treasury of wisdom which needs to be prized and shared since it offers healing strength providing inspiration for creative action in times of stress.

Here in these pages we seek to share with you a portion of this ancient and modern wealth. You will find expressions of a love of life which stretches back more than five thousand years, but the spirit is contemporary. These prayers of power are from Akhnaton as well as Maya Angelou, Chief Yellow Lark as well as T. S. Eliot, Robert Frost as well as Francis of Assisi, the Upanishads as well as the Psalms, Reinhold Niebuhr as well as May Sarton. Potent healing words flow from the spirit of Starhawk, Jane Austen and Sojourner Truth, Dorothy Sayers and the Medical Mission Sisters, Howard Thurman, Henry David Thoreau, and Walt Whitman.

People's creative responses to crises in their lives are what we editors have found precious for our own health and healing. Through many years while serving as chaplains and ministers—often focused on personal, national and international issues—we have found prayer both necessary and invaluable for maintaining our own buoyancy and balance. Each social problem requires both personal poise and the courage to act with wisdom.

Here we share with you a small group of the most helpful prayers which we have discovered and prized. The emphasis throughout is on world affirmation and reverence for life. Wherever necessary all these prayers of power have been degenderized. Archaic language is avoided. While the accent falls on twentieth century works of North America, many centuries and many continents are represented in this search for inner ways of making the world whole again.

H. F. V.
Cambridge, Massachusetts 2008

PRAYERS

AKHNATON.

THE STRENGTH OF THE EARTH

O living Source of Power,
Beautiful is Your dawning.

When You arise in the East,
You fill each land with beauty.

Glittering high above every land,
Your greatness is visible to all.

Though You are far away,
Your rays are upon the Earth.

Though You are high,
Your footprints are the day.

When You arise on the horizon,
You drive the darkness away.

When You send forth Your rays,
The lands are in daily festivity.

When You awaken them,
The cattle stand on their feet.

The trees and plants flourish;
Birds sing along the river.

All the animals dance on their feet
When You shine on them.

Your rays nourish every garden
As You make things live and grow.

Dawning, glittering, going and returning,
You make the season's millions of forms.

Tribes and towns and cities all see You,
For You are the Strength of the Earth.

ALCUIN

ETERNAL ONE

Eternal Light, shine into our hearts;
Eternal Goodness, deliver us from evil;
Eternal Power, be our support;
Eternal Wisdom, scatter the darkness of our ignorance:
That we may seek Your face
With all our heart and mind and soul and strength.

AMERICAN BOOK OF COMMON PRAYER

FOR THE POOR AND NEGLECTED

Almighty God, we remember before You all poor and neglected persons, whom it would be easy to forget: the homeless and the destitute; the old and the sick who have none to care for them. May Your goodness rest upon them. Help us to heal those who are broken in body or spirit, and to turn their sorrow to joy; to lift up the downhearted and cheer them with hope. When they are perplexed and troubled, may Your presence save them from despair.

AMERICAN STUDENT HYMNAL

LABOR

Worker of the world, we are thankful for those about us whose labor
    enhances our lives day by day:
For men and women who face peril and suffer pain;
For those who fill the earth and tend machinery;
For those who strive in deep waters and venture in far countries;
For those who work in offices and warehouses;
For those who labor at furnaces and in factories;
For those who toil in mines and in space;
For those who buy and sell;
For those who care for children and families;
For all who live by strength of arm and hand;
For all who manage and govern;
For all who enrich the common life through the arts and sciences;
    For all who teach and communicate;
And for all who serve the common good as religious leaders,
    physicians, lawyers, engineers, librarians, social workers, and
    diplomats.
We are thankful for all whose labor enhances our lives.

4

LANCELOT ANDREWES

BE ALL TO ALL

We bring before You, O God:
    the cries of the weary,
    the pains of the distressed,
    the tears of the tragedies of life,
    the anxious hours of the insecure,
    the restlessness of the refugees,
    the hunger of the oppressed.
Dear God, be near to each.

Helper of the helpless,
Hope of the homeless,
The Strength of those tossed with tempests,
The Haven of those who sail:
Be all to all.

Be within us, to strengthen us;
    without us, to keep us;
    above us, to inspire us;
    beneath us, to uphold us;
    before us, to direct us;
    behind us , to propel us;
    around us, to sustain us.
Be all to all in present need.

MAYA ANGELOU

THANK YOU, GOD

I want to thank You, God,
For life and all that's in it.
Thank You for the day
And for the hour and for the minute.
I know many are gone;
I'm still living on.
I want to thank You.

ANONYMOUS

ALL THAT WE HAVE

Almighty God, Giver of every good and perfect gift, teach us to render unto You all that we have and all that we are, that we may praise You not with our lips only but with our whole lives, turning the sorrows and the joys of each successive day into a living contribution to Your life.

STRENGTH

God of our days and our nights, brace us and hearten us as we face our daily duties. In our hours of weariness and discouragement, You save us from self-pity. In our moments of achievement, You keep us unassuming and humble. So may we worthily fulfill our tasks and meet the duties of our day.

THE LIGHTING OF THE CANDLES

Lest we forget the great traditions of freedom and faith which are the heritage of humanity; lest we forget the pioneers, the statesmen, the bridge builders, the artists; and lest we forget You, the God of our forebears who is our God also:
We light this candle of remembrance.
For the hope of a better world, in which righteousness and peace shall prevail among the people of the earth, and to create which is the task of the generations in which we stand, as well as for the courage and faith we shall need if we are to carry on this unfinished work:
We light this candle of consecration.
May the flame upon the altar of free faith shine in our hearts always, reminding us of the dark places to which we may carry light and strengthening us in every moment of doubt and discouragement with unwavering faith in You whom we serve and whose we are.

THE PRAYER OF A PARENT

Now that the children are asleep, dear God, I am tired and would spend a half hour in stillness.
May my burning heart feel Your ever-renewing power. May I not be unduly annoyed by the little things of life. You give me a large view, a sense of proportion, so I can truly judge what is important, what is not.
I turn to You for strength to be a fine parent to my children, knowing how to help them to unfold their dreams as well as to care for their bodies. May they grow up healthy, creatively affirming life.

SLOW US DOWN...YET ALSO

Slow us down, O God. Ease the pounding of our hearts by the quieting of our minds;

Yet also, wake us up. Shake the complacency out of our souls by opening our minds to the cry of the wounded, the refugees wandering without homes, the homeless at home, and the children who starve.

Steady our hurried pace with a vision of the eternal reach of time;

Yet also, quicken our steps with a vision of the urgent action now required to cure the causes of stunted growth, premature death, battered women, and abused children.

Give us, amid the confusion of the day, the calmness of the everlasting hills;

Yet also, alert our eyes not to the comforting illusion of constancy divorced from change, but rather to such sharp reality as deep poverty surrounding us at home and abroad.

Break the tensions of our nerves and muscles with the soothing music of the singing streams;

Yet also, give us, amid the calm days of our years, souls which are prepared to cope with the confusion necessarily occurring amidst new creation in the cities, towns, and the countries of the earth.

Help us to know the magical, restoring power of sleep;

Yet also, break the chains of euphoria deluding us to think that we are acting responsibly when we do no more than listen to music which protects our feet from marching.

Remind us of the fable of the hare and the tortoise, that we may know that there is more to life than increasing its speed;

Yet also, remind us of the fable of the astrologer who fell plumb to the bottom of a well, not seeing his feet while reading the sky.

Slow us down, O God, and inspire us to send our roots deep into the soil of life's enduring values, that we may grow more surely toward the stars;

Yet also, wake us up, so our eyes may see the people around us and our arms may be open to embrace the suffering who cry.

ANSELM

WE BRING OUR TROUBLES

We bring before You, O God:
The troubles and perils of people and nations,

The sighings of the sick,
The sorrows of the bereaved,
The necessities of strangers,
The helplessness of the weak,
The despondency of the weary,
The failing powers of any age.

May each of us draw as near to You
As You are near to each of us.

MARCUS AURELIUS

UNTO THE UNIVERSE

O Universe, from You are all things; to You all things return.

WALDEMAR ARGOW

FOR WISDOM

Everliving Source of us all,
May we find wisdom this day;
May we come to understand —
that we without You are a well without water;
that a person without friends is a tree without branches;
that words without deeds are a cry no one can hear;
that knowing without feeling is a head without a body;
that strength without tenderness is a darkness where no light shines;
that life without love is a desert where no rain falls.

May the wisdom we find this day make us wiser in the days ahead:
Wise enough to be ourselves and to try to understand ourselves as best
    we may;
Wise enough to be the master of our moods;
Wise enough to find in the buffeting and shocks of life a discipline that
    will make us stronger than we were before.

May the varied experiences of each day increase our store of wisdom.
May our fellowship with one another, and with You, increase our trea-
    sury of love

ARISTOPHANES

ELIXIR OF NATIONS

From the murmur and subtlety of suspicion with which we vex one another, give us rest.

Make a new beginning, and mingle again the kindred of nations in the alchemy of love; and with some fine essence of forbearance, temper our minds.

AUGUSTINE

OUR HEARTS ARE RESTLESS

Everlasting God, in whom we live and move and have our being: You have made us for Yourself, and hearts are restless until they rest in You.

YOU ARE MY HEALTH

Great are You, O God, and greatly to be praised; great is Your power, and Your wisdom infinite. We who are but a particle of Your creation, praise You. You awaken us to delight in Your praise; for You made us for Yourself, and our hearts are restless until they rest in You.

What are You then, my God? Most high, most good, most omnipotent; most merciful, yet most just; most hidden, yet most present; most beautiful, yet most strong; stable, yet incomprehensible; unchangeable, yet all-changing; ever old, ever new; supporting, filling, and overspreading; creating, flourishing, and maturing; seeking, yet having all things. You, O God, are my life, my joy, my health.

A PERSONAL PRAYER

O God, the Light of the heart that sees You,
The Life of the soul that loves You,
The Strength of the mind that seeks You:
May I ever continue to be steadfast in Your love.

Be the joy of my heart;
Take all of me to Yourself, and abide therein.

The house of my soul is, I confess, too narrow for You.
Enlarge it that You may enter.
It is ruinous, but do repair it.
It has within it what must offend Your eyes;
I confess and know it,
But whose help shall I seek in cleansing it but Yours alone?

To You, O God, I cry urgently.
Cleanse me from secret faults.
Keep me from false pride and sensuality
That they not get dominion over me.

A PERSONAL INVOCATION

O Love of God, descend into my heart;
Enlighten the dark corners of this neglected dwelling,
And scatter there Your cheerful beams.
Dwell in the soul that longs to be Your temple;
Water that barren soil overrun with weeds and briars
And lost for lack of cultivating.
Make it fruitful with Your dew.

Come, dear Refreshment of those who languish;
Come, Star and Guide of those who sail amidst tempests.
You are the Haven of the tossed and shipwrecked.
Come now, Glory and Crown of the living,
As well as the Safeguard of the dying.
Come, Sacred Spirit;
Come, and fit me to receive You.

JOHN BAILLIE

THE HEAVY LADEN

O God, we bring before You the burden of the world's life:
       All who are far from home and friends,
       All who lie down hungry or cold,
       All who suffer pain,
       All who are kept awake by anxiety,
       All who are facing danger,
       All who toil, or keep watch while others sleep.
May they have a sense of Your presence that will turn their
loneliness into comfort and their trouble into peace.

KARLE WILSON BAKER

PRONOUNS

O God, You said,
"Say, 'We'";
But I shook my head,
Hid my hands tight behind my back, and said,
Stubbornly,
"I."

Again You said,
"Say, 'We'";
But I looked upon them, grimy and all awry.
Myself in those twisted shapes? Ah, no!
Distastefully I turned my head away,
Persisting,
"They."

Again You said,
"Say, 'We'";
And I
At last,
Richer by a hoard
Of years,
Looked in their eyes and found the heavy word
That bent my neck and bowed my head:
Like a shamed school child then I mumbled low,
"We, O God."

JOSEPH BARTH

A GRACE

We give thanks for Being;
We give thanks for being here;
We give thanks for being here together.

BEACON SONG AND SERVICE BOOK

THE WORK OF THE WORLD

Wondrous giver of all things, this world is full of Your riches. We thank You for the splendor of nature and for Your bountiful provision for our human needs. May we not waste Your gifts nor needlessly ignore the welfare of others in our use of them. We seek to do our part in the work of the world, and so enter into fellowship with all who toil and all who create. We would recognize the right of every human being to share in what You give. We would help to make our planet a true home for all of Your children, where each may have an equal opportunity both for work and for the rewards of work.

LUDWIG VAN BEETHOVEN

GIVE ME STRENGTH

O God, give me strength to be victorious over myself. Guide my spirit; raise me from these dark depths that my soul, transported through Your wisdom, may fearlessly struggle in fiery flight; for You alone understand and You alone can inspire me.

ONE THING MORE

We praise Your goodness that You have left nothing undone to draw us to Yourself; but one thing we ask of You, O God; that You not cease Your work in our improvement. Let us tend toward You, no matter by what means, and be fruitful in good works.

STEPHEN VINCENT BENÉT

A COMMON FAITH

God of the free, our Earth is small in the great universe. Grant us the wisdom and the vision to comprehend the greatness of the human spirit that suffers and endures hugely for a goal beyond our own brief span.

We are all children of the Earth. Grant us that simple knowledge. If others are oppressed, then we are oppressed. If they hunger, we hunger. If their freedom is taken away, our freedom is not secure. Grant us a common faith that we shall know bread and peace, freedom and security, an equal opportunity to do our best, not only in our own lands, but throughout the world. In that faith, let us march toward the clean world our hands can make.

BOOK OF COMMON PRAYER

FORGIVE US, O GOD

Forgive, O God, those national sins which so easily beset us: our wanton waste of soil and air and water; our desecration of natural beauty; our heedlessness of those who come after us, if only we be served; our lust for money; our contempt for what is small and worship of what is big. For wrongs done to our land, our people, our heritage, and our future, as well as for things left undone, forgive us, O God.

ANNE BRADSTREET

MY WINTER'S PAST

As spring the winter does succeed,
And leaves the naked trees do dress,
The earth all black is clothed in green;
At sunshine each their joy express.

My sun's returned with healing wings.
My soul and body do rejoice;
My heart exults and praises sings
To You who heard my wailing voice.

My winter's past, my storms are gone,
And former clouds now seem all fled;
But, if they must eclipse again,
I'll run where I was amply fed.

I have a shelter from the storm,
A shadow from the fainting heat;
I have access unto Your throne
You who are God so wondrous great.

MARGUERITE HARMON BRO

FOR TREES

We thank You for trees, O God. We thank You for the trees of our childhood in whose shade we played and read and dreamed. We thank You for special trees which will always stand large in our memory because they became our trees. We thank You for great stretches of trees which make the forests, drawing sustenance from Your bounties of sun and water, earth and air, even as we draw strength from them.

ROBERT BURNS

THE SELKIRK GRACE

Some hae meat, and canna eat,
And some wad eat that want it;
But we hae meat, and we can eat,
And sae our God be thank it!

CHIEF YELLOW LARK

I COME BEFORE YOU

Great Spirit, whose voice I hear in the winds and whose breath gives life to the world: as I come before You, one of Your many children, I am small and weak; I need Your strength and wisdom. May I walk in beauty; may my eyes behold the red and purple sunset; may my hands respect what You have made; may my ears be sharp to hear Your voice.

Make me wise, so I may know what You teach in every leaf and rock. Make me strong, so I may be able to fight my greatest enemy, myself. May I ever be ready to come to You with clean hands and straight eyes, so that when life fades like a sunset, I may come You without shame.

MAX COOTS

A HARVEST OF PEOPLE

Let us give thanks for a bounty of people:

For generous friends, with smiles as bright as their blossoms.
For feisty friends as tart as apples;
For continuous friends who, like scallions and cucumbers, keep reminding us that we've had them.
For crotchety friends, as sour as rhubarb and as indestructible;
For handsome friends, who are as gorgeous as eggplants and as elegant as a row of corn; and the others as plain as potatoes and as good for you.
For friends as unpretentious as cabbages, as subtle as summer squash, as persistent as parsley, as endless as zucchini, and who, like parsnips, can be counted on to see you through the winter.
For old friends, nodding like sunflowers in the evening-time.
For young friends, who wind around like tendrils and hold us.

We give thanks for friends now gone, like gardens past that have been harvested, but who fed us in their times that we might live.

J. RAYMOND COPE

YOU WHO ARE ONE

O God, we rejoice to find in our search that:
You are the Truth clouded by our ignorance;
You are the Beauty in whose light we are joyfully alive;
You are the Goodness invincible amidst and above evil;
You are the Will deeper than our own wills;
You are the Love that slowly raises the human soul;
You are the Eternal in which all that is Temporal is rooted;
You are our Beginning and our End;
You are the Object of our life's quest;
You are the Inspiration for the quest itself;
You are to be found both without and within.

In our search, give us courage and strength, patience and confidence,
O You who are One-in-All

SPIRIT OF LIFE

Spirit of Life that is within us and about us: in each of us there is
some margin of despair and hope, some overtone of creation's song; in
each of us the welling ache of life; the being and the becoming; the promise and the hunger; the one resurgent moment that speaks of eternity,
that may pass from memory but is never forgotten.

In each of us there is some margin of discovery; some truant shadow
of tomorrow; in each of us, an un-named need, a purpose brooding and
uncertain, waiting to be realized.

Spirit of Life that is within us and about us: we rededicate ourselves
to a higher purpose, a nobler dream, a more perfect life together nourished in wisdom and love.

SAMUEL McCHORD CROTHERS

THE ETERNAL NOW

Eternal Power moving through our very life this moment, we rejoice in
Your working through the ages. As we are mindful of Your deathless power in us, may our work and our worship become one. May we be mindful
of our being co-creators with You in this fathomless Universe, which is
our home. Scarcely can we see the height, depth, length and breadth of
Your love, which unites us with ancient and emerging stars, as well as with
ancient and emerging cells. Through Your strength, we seek to enlarge our
view of the life of ages flowing in our own lives this very moment and
forever.

e. e. cummings

i thank You God

i thank You God for most this amazing
day: for the leaping greenly spirits of trees
and a blue true dream of sky; and for everything
which is natural which is infinite which is yes

(i who have died am alive again today,
and this is the sun's birthday; this is the birth
day of life and of love and wings: and of the gay
great happening illimitably earth)

how should tasting touching hearing seeing
breathing any—lifted from the no
of all nothing—human merely being
doubt unimaginable You?

(now the ears of my ears awake and
now the eyes of my eyes are opened)

DADU

PLAY OF CREATION

O this beauty of the universe!
How do You, O God, continue to create it?
What burst of ecstasy
Allows You to manifest Your being?
Some say You take fancy in the play of form.
I understand You need participants like me
In Your perpetual play of creation.

A. POWELL DAVIES

WALLS

Eternal Spirit, life of our minds and breath of our being: strangely
do we walk though the days of our years, unseeing, unhearing, inattentive, though the glory of life is all about us. We wrap ourselves up in the
petty and trivial, shutting out life's promise. We are afraid of life—and its
mighty claim upon us—and we wall ourselves in, thinking to be safe.

Break down our walls, O God! Blow upon the barriers we have built
to keep us paltry. Let them all be swept away!

IF WE COME TO YOU

Eternal Spirit, who dwells in the hearts of those who seek You: if we come to You in joy, may we draw strength from the experience; if we come in sorrow, touch us with Your great compassion; if we have lost our way, and the darkness has overtaken us, may the light of Your presence appear before us that we may see our path; if we come to You weak and discouraged and know not where to turn, may we recall the resources You have given us. Illumine our minds with a vision of the future's promise.

DISCOVERY

Eternal Spirit, who gives wisdom, show us how much of what we pray for in the world about us is waiting to be found within ourselves.

PRAYERS

Give us to know, O God, how vain are all our hopes, how empty all our prayers, until we ourselves are ready to fulfill them.

THE FRESHNESS OF CREATION

God of the morning of the world, at the sound of whose voice creation wakes and sings, open our hearts to the gladness of the earth. May the freshness of creation cleanse our souls. Forgive us that we go on our way in haste. Lift up our eyes! May we see the wonder all about us, from the most fragile petal on the tiniest of blooms to the miracle of a new blade of grass. We thank You for this revelation of Yourself that never grows old. May the beauty of Your world breathe into our spirits.

BREATHE YET AGAIN

How can we come to You, O God, with hearts that we have closed to one another?

O Holy One, remind us! We are Your children, all, lighted by the same precarious flame. How foolish are our walls of prejudice, our empty pride!

O patient God, take pity on us! You who breathed into us the one breath of our common life, breathe yet again, and bring us to our souls' awakening.

HOW LONG, O GOD?

How long must it be, O God—for our years grow shorter—before we are ready for our duty? All about us are the miseries of human injustice and oppression. When shall we be one with the destitute, the dispossessed, opening our hearts to the downcast and the weary? These are flesh of our flesh, bearing Your image and breathing Your breath within them. They are pilgrims with us, one in hope and yearning. O God, when we pray for a better world, joyous and peaceful, with all its banners bright, help us to see that we ourselves must bring this world to pass, and take us to where our work is waiting for us.

GRATITUDE AND FORTITUDE

In our ever changing world so full of what is wonderful, help us, O God, to accept with gratitude all that gladdens us, and to accept with fortitude all that brings us grief.

May we take time to watch the morning and the evening skies, to look often and long at the marvellous earth and all that lives upon it, to be with heart and soul a friend and neighbor and a part of humankind.

We rejoice in the heritage bequeathed to us from yesterday as we celebrate festivals of faith and hope.

May we be learning always, from all that we see and do, and from all that happens to us;' and if shadows overtake us, may we not dim within ourselves the light that helps others to live.

MY SORROW

The love I can no longer give to my beloved, help me, O God, to give to those who need it. Save me from frozenness of heart! Make my compassion deeper, my sympathy wider. Melt away my bitterness, and let my sorrow teach me to be gentle. If so much that is precious can so soon be lost, let me cherish what remains; and let me be the nurturer of things precious in the lives of others.

EXPECTATIONS

May we remember, O God, that from those to whom much has been given, much is expected.

TIME AND TIMELESSNESS

O God of timeless ages, in whom the past, the present, and the future meet: we bow our heads before the everlasting. Our years come and go swiftly. Soon we children of an hour must give back to You the breath that gave us life. Yet the voice of faith sings in our nighttime. The silence speaks; the darkness glows. Amid the haste, we see the march of destinies and feel Your presence as our dust is lighted with immortal power.

NOT IN THE CLOVEN SKIES

O God, the quest of ages, found and lost and sought anew in every generation: may we understand more plainly what it means to seek Your presence. We heard that You would come in splendor, cleaving the skies, but this we know is but a dream. O God, may we amend our seeking, for we ourselves know better. We have heard You speak wherever truth is spoken; we have seen You in life's loveliness; we have felt Your presence in all brave and generous deeds. We would find You where You are, O God, in our daily common life.

THE HOPE

O God, when the shame of what we are is upon us, touch us with the hope of our becoming.

PRAY SOFTLY

O God, when we thank You for what is given to us and not to others, let us remember to pray softly, for there will be many who overhear.

THE GREATER LOSS

When we remember, O God, those we have loved and lost, we remember also that not to have loved would have been far greater loss.

DIONYSIUS OF ALEXANDRIA

PEACE

Great God, the sacred One-in-All,
Good beyond all that is good,
Fair beyond all that is fair,
In whom are calmness and peace.

Make up the dissensions which divide us from each other.
Bring us back to a unity of love
Which bears some likeness to Your sublime nature.

As You are one amidst and above all events,
Make us one through the unanimity of a sound mind,
That through the embrace of love,
We may be spiritually one,
As well in ourselves as in each other,
By that peace of Yours which makes all things peaceful.

W. E. B. DUBOIS

PRAYER

In these first beginnings of the new life of the world, renew in us the resolution to persist in the good work we have begun. Give us strength of body and strength of mind and the unfaltering determination to carry out that which we know to be good and right. Forgive all wavering in the past service of Thy cause and make us strong to go forward in spite of the doubts of our friends and our enemies and in spite of our own distrust in ourselves. Out of the death of winter comes ever and again the resurrection of spring: so out of evil bring good, O God, and out of doubt determination. Amen.

EGYPTIAN HYMN

PRAISE BE TO YOU

Praise be to You, O God, the oldest Existence, the Support of all that is, the Maker of herbs and animals and us; indeed, Maker of all happenings within and above and below us; Deliverer of the suffering and oppressed; Source of joy; You whose name is hidden:

Praise be to You, Sleepless One; praise from the creatures of every land ,as well as from the height of heaven to the depth of the sea.

We extol You; we worship You.

ELGIN CATHEDRAL EPITAPH

EPITAPH

Here lie I, Martin Elginbrodde:

Have mercy on my soul, O God,

As I would do, if I were God,

And You were Martin Elginbrodde.

THOMAS STEARNS ELIOT

CHORUS X

O Light Invisible, we praise You!
Too bright for mortal vision.
O Greater Light, we praise You for the less;
The eastern light our spires touch at morning,
The light that slants upon our western doors at evening,
The twilight over stagnant pools at batflight,
Moon light and star light, owl and moth light,
Glow-worm glowlight on a grassblade.
O Light Invisible, we worship You!

We thank You for the lights that we have kindled,
The light of altar and of sanctuary;
Small lights of those who meditate at midnight
And lights directed through the colored panes of windows
And light reflected from the polished stone,
The gilded carven wood, the colored fresco.
Our gaze is submarine, our eyes look upward
And see the light that fractures through unquiet water.
We see the light but see not whence it comes.
O Light Invisible, we glorify You!

In our rhythm of earthly life, we tire of light.
We are glad when the day ends, when the play ends; and ecstasy is
     too much pain.
We are children quickly tired: children who are up in the night and
     fall asleep as the rocket is fired; and the day is long for work or
     play.
We tire of distraction or concentration, we sleep and are glad to
     sleep,
Controlled by the rhythm of blood and the day and the night and the
     seasons.
And we must extinguish the candle, put out the light and relight it;
Forever must quench, forever relight the flame.
Therefore we thank You for our little light, that is dappled with shad-
     ow.
We thank You who has moved us to building, to finding, to forming
     at the ends of our fingers and beams of our eyes.
And when we have built an altar to the Invisible Light, we may set
     thereon the little lights for which our bodily vision is made.
And we thank You that darkness reminds us of light.
O Light Invisible, we give You thanks for Your great glory!

AN ENGLISH COMMON PRAYER

WE GIVE THANKS

We give thanks, O God for the wonder of creation, for the gifts of human life and fellowship.

For the wisdom of leaders in diverse fields, for their strength and courage to carry out the duties of their various callings;

For the administrators of local, national, and international governments, that they may act with discernment amidst the crises of our time, moderating racial and social conflicts;

For those in industry and commerce, in trade and business, for mutual care and cooperation;

For exemplars of art and music, theater and entertainment, sport and leisure, in recognition of gifts given to one another;

For every mode of communication, in literature and press, movies and film, radio and television, telephone, computer, and advancing forms of telecommunication across the planet and in space in the service of truth;

For education in family and school, college and university, at work and everywhere encouraging maturity and fulfillment of life.

For the service of those in sickness and need, anxiety and suffering, actions expressing a community that cares, we give thanks now and evermore.

EPICTETUS

GREAT ARE YOU

Great are You, O God:

That is the hymn our hearts would sing as we dig and plough and eat. At every moment, we would sing these praises and, above all, the greatest and divinest praise: that You have given us the power to comprehend these gifts and to walk in the way of reason.

If I were a nightingale, I should sing as a nightingale; if a swan, as a swan; but as I am a rational human being, I must praise You, O Deathless Power, forever and ever.

ARTHUR FOOTE II

FOR COURAGE

O God whom we know but long to know better, You who are the depth of our own being and the mysterious Other whom we encounter:

Ours is a prayer for courage, the courage to be ourselves; the courage to face reality, to accept the uncertainty of the future and the fact of our mortality. May we have the courage to doubt and the courage to doubt our doubts. When our lives are like a house of cards that threatens to collapse, grant us strength to step into the dark singing a bold song of trust in You.

Ours is a prayer for self-acceptance. Increase our hunger to know the truth, the whole truth about ourselves; for we know we cannot defeat the evil in us so long as we pretend it is not there. Unmask our hidden hostilities. Teach us to recognize our forbidden desires. Help us to accept our whole selves.

Ours is a prayer for love. We pray to be more able to love, to give love as well as to receive it. May our confession of how critical and judgmental we are be a first step on our journey toward becoming white corpuscles fighting the infections of prejudice and hatred which threaten our whole world.

To our spoken words of prayer, we add the unspoken desires and longings of our hearts to find You, the Source of all good that causes us to pray for courage, for self-acceptance, and for love.

OPEN OUR LIVES

O Love that holds our souls in life, we confess the inconstancy of our lives: our contentment with mediocrity, our timidity in speaking, our uncharitableness.

Locked behind doors of fear-filled self-concern, we pray to be able to draw back every bolt and bar, that there may be openness and light and joy in all our being.

We would open our eyes to all the wonder of Your order, to the glory of color and shape, to the strength in ordinary children and youth, men and women, to the sublimities of the human story, and to all such intimations of Your presence.

We would open our ears to all the varied music of the world: the melodies of human voices, the swelling harmonies of many instruments, and all the music not made by us: the songs of wind and bird, the thunder's timpani, the rhythms of running water.

We would also open our ears to the still sad music of humanity: the falling of our tears, the woe of our hearts.

We would open our minds for new thoughts, the weighing of new evidence welcoming what challenges our complacency and prejudice, proving all things.

23

We would open our hands, ready to share Your bounty, freeing ourselves from miserly clutching and from grasping at life as though You had not provided abundantly for all our needs.

We would open our lips, not in foolish words and much speaking, but to utter the courageous word when people are downhearted, the sympathetic word when they are suffering.

Open our lips, O God, that our mouths may show forth Your praise.

FRANCIS OF ASSISI

THE CANTICLE OF THE SUN

O Most High, Almighty God: to You belong praise, glory, honor, and all blessing.

Praise be to You with all Your creatures: and especially our brother the sun, who brings us the day and who brings us the light. Fair is he and shining with a very great splendor: O God, to us he signifies You.

Praise be to You for our sister the moon, and for the stars which You have set clear and lovely in the heavens.

Praise be to You for our brother the wind, and for air and cloud, calms and all weather, by which You uphold in life all creatures.

Praise be to You for our sister water, who is very serviceable unto us, and humble and precious and clean.

Praise be to You for our brother fire, through whom You give light in the darkness; and he is bright and pleasant, and very mighty and strong.

Praise be to You for our mother, the earth, which sustains us and keeps us, and brings forth diverse fruits, and flowers of many colors, and grass.

Praise be to You for all those who pardon one another for love's sake, and who endure weakness and tribulation.

Blessed are they who peaceably shall endure, for You, O Most High, shall give them a crown.

Praise be to You for our sister the death of the body, from whom no one escapes.

We praise and bless and give thanks to You, O God, and serve You with great humility.

MAKE ME AN INSTRUMENT OF YOUR PEACE

God, make me an instrument of Your peace.
Where there is hatred, let me sow love;
Where there is injury, pardon;
Where there is doubt, faith;
Where there is despair, hope;
Where there is darkness, light;
Where there is sadness, joy.

Great Friend,
May I not so much seek to be consoled as to console;
To be understood as to understand;
To be loved as to love.
For it is in giving that we receive;
It is in pardoning that we are pardoned;
And it is in dying that we are born to eternal life.

STEPHEN H. FRITCHMAN

TO ALL WHO TOIL

Spirit of Truth and Love within our living hearts, we pledge our faithfulness to all who toil that we may eat our bread. We rejoice in human power to shape the stuff of earth into things of usefulness and beauty. May our hands and minds add their portion to the common treasure of a world more fair. We would find our place among the workers of humanity, proud of honest labor done, and rest deserved, and wages earned. We would pay our tribute to the task well done of tailor, teacher, carpenter, and nurse; of surgeon, painter, sailor, chemist, housewife, typist, farmer and chef; and for all of those whose work is little known and rarely seen, yet daily given, that our lives may be far happier and safe. May this be a time of kinship among the toilers of every race and clime.

ROBERT FROST

A PRAYER IN SPRING

Oh, give us pleasure in the flowers to-day;
And give us not to think so far away
As the uncertain harvest; keep us here
All simply in the springing of the year.

Oh, give us pleasure in the orchard white,
Like nothing else by day, like ghosts by night;
And make us happy in the happy bees,
The swarm dilating round the perfect trees.

And make us happy in the darting bird
That suddenly above the bees is heard,
The meteor that thrusts in with needle bill,
And off a blossom in mid air stands still.

For this is love and nothing else is love,
The which it is reserved for You above
To sanctify to what far ends You will,
But which it only needs that we fulfil.

MAX GAEBLER

GREAT SPIRIT

Great Spirit, the Life of all our being, the Light of all our seeing, the Strength of all our striving, the Love of all our living: we rejoice that You are invisible, yet You are round about all of us and in each of us. We would open every window of our being to the intaking and outgiving of Your breath of life, until each one of us is born anew, filled with Your mighty and mysterious presence.

GAELIC PRAYER

ANCIENT BLESSING

May the blessing of light be on you, light without and light within. May the blessed Sunlight shine on you and warm your heart until it glows, so that a stranger may come and be warmed by it, and also a friend. May the light shine out of the two eyes of you like a candle set in two windows of a house, bidding the wanderer to come in out of the storm.

May the blessing of the Rain be on you—soft, sweet rain. May it fall upon your spirit so that flowers may spring up. And may the Great Rains be on you. May they beat upon your spirit and wash it fair and clean, and leave there many a shining pool where the blue of heaven shines reflected, and sometimes a star.

May the blessing of the Earth be on you—the great and round earth. May you have a kindly greeting for folks you pass as you're going along the roads. May the earth be soft under you when you lie upon it, tired at the close of the day.

FRED GILLIS

MEDITATION ON MANY PLACES

We come from many places seeking a center for our lives, a sense of wholeness.

We come from dry places where the words and the knowledge seem broken into brittle fragments that do not cohere.

We come from overfilled places where information abounds, but there is no real understanding.

We come from hard places where feelings are dulled, hollow places where meanings seem empty.

Now, at this time of quiet reflection, we come to be emptied and filled with life's Spirit that flows in and among us and through the world.

Empty us of the clatter and confusion, the information we thought all-sufficient.

Quiet our minds; center our spirits; ground our being.

Enable us to find Your power that is already within us, power for love, creativity, hope.

Open our eyes to the sustenance that already surrounds and up-holds us.

Help us to see the miracle of life in each moment and each cubic inch of space offering a gift of opportunity.

May our minds be open to wisdom, our spirits open to grace.

JOAN GOODWIN

TO THE FOUR DIRECTIONS

Spirit of the East, spirit of air, of morning and springtime: Be with us as the sun rises, in times of beginning, times of planting. Inspire us with the fresh breath of courage as we go forth into new adventures.

Spirit of the South, spirit of fire, of noontime and summer: Be with us through the heat of the day and help us to be ever growing. Warm us with strength and energy for the work that awaits.

Spirit of the West, spirit of water, of evening and autumn: Be with us as the sun sets, and help us to enjoy a rich harvest. Flow through us with a cooling, healing quietness and bring us peace.

Spirit of the North, spirit of earth, of nighttime and winter: Be with us in the darkness, in the time of gestation. Ground us in the wisdom of the changing seasons as we celebrate the spiraling journey of our lives.

GEORGIA HARKNESS

THE AGONY OF GOD

I listen to Your agony, O God;
I who am fed,
Who never yet went hungry for a day.
I see the dead,
The children starved for lack of bread;
I see and try to pray.

I listen to Your agony, O God;
I who am warm,
Who never yet have lacked a sheltered home.
In dull alarm,
The dispossessed of hut and farm
Aimless and transient roam.

I listen to Your agony, O God;
I who am strong,
With health and love and laughter in my soul.
I see a throng
Of stunted children reared in wrong
And yearn to make them whole.

I listen to Your agony, O God;
But know full well
That not until I share their bitter cry,
Earth's pain and hell,
Can You within my spirit dwell
To bring Your kingdom nigh.

DONALD S. HARRINGTON

STRENGTH FOR THE DAY

We thank You, O God, for the cheerfulness which has broken into the darkness of our self-made dungeons; for the way in which old misunderstandings may fade away and old quarrels be washed out by compassion; for the insurgent courage which ever lifts its head above the roaring cross currents of past mistakes and miseries and affirms the age-old right to try again.

JOHN F. HAYWARD

FOR SONG

Source of our singing and Perfect Receiver of our offering of song, we rejoice with thanksgiving. All creatures offer praise with rejoicing; all creatures suffer hurt and make plaintive music of their misery. We ask for no single tone of life: we know that tone and time must ever change, sometimes bitter, sometimes serene, but we pray that the singing may never end; that bright songs and sad songs may arise from the fountain of our lives all our days. In the first cries of infancy, in the songs of childhood, in the music of our years of strength, and in the voices of our oldest age, we offer our thanksgiving unto You, the Master Singer, the Eternal Music.

GERALD HEARD

TIDES OF JOY

Fathomless Ocean of Love, ever creating the universe anew: give us grace to go about all our doings cheerfully, rhythmically, with hearts lifted high, knowing that no matter how troubled the surface water of life seem to be, we are constantly upheld by Your deep tides of joy.

LIFE'S DIVINE DANCE

God of the universe, who calls us to participate in life's divine dance, we would trustingly swing into the unfolding design of life. At every inner prompting of Your spirit, may we forget ourselves in unhesitating desire to help fulfill Your creative purposes.

DAY BY DAY

O God, as we acknowledge that every good thing comes from You, we pray we may practice day by day:
> Humility without despair,
> Trust without conceit,
> Love without jealousy,
> Strength without domination,
> Gentleness without weakness.

RALPH N. HELVERSON

FRAGMENT OF A PRAYER

Be with those today who bear burdens too heavy to be borne alone. In the myriad ways we may live our lives, enable us to find strength to do our duty. For those who bear the weight of illness, often unknown to others, sustain and uphold. For those who bear a scar in the soul torturing and searing the inner life, bring unity and peace. For those who stand at the brink of some momentous decision, bring clarity and inner resolution. For those who walk in the shadow of fear, bring wisdom. God of our secret and open quest for significance and strength, be with us and in us and around us.

FRANK HOLMES

THE EVERLASTING WAR

Let me not cry, "Peace, peace!" when there should be no peace in the everlasting war of the better against the worse.

Let me not accept as inevitable any unnecessary suffering, or cry, "Impossible!" before the dream of a more just world.

Keep alive within me this day, O God, the sacred flame of indignation. Help me to say, "No!" to what is inhumane, that by my word and courage the forces of fairness may be strengthened in my time.

GERARD MANLEY HOPKINS

GOD'S GRANDEUR

The world is charged with Your grandeur, O God.
    It will flame out, like shining from shook foil;
    It gathers to a greatness, like the ooze of oil
Crushed. Why do we then now not reck Your rod?
Generations have trod, have trod, have trod;
    And all is seared with trade; bleared smeared with toil;
    And sears our smudge and shares our smell: the soil
Is bare now, nor can foot feel, being shod.

And for all this, nature is never spent;
    There lives the dearest freshness deep down things;
And though the last lights off the black West went
    Oh, morning, at the brown brink eastward, springs—
Because Your Holy Power over the bent
    World broods with warm breast and with ah! bright wings

PIED BEAUTY

Glory be, O God, for dappled things—
    For skies of couple-color as a brindled cow;
        For rose-moles all in stipple upon trout that swim;
Fresh firecoal chestnut-falls; finches wings;
    Landscapes plotted and pieced—fold, fallow, and plough;
        And all trades, their gear and tackle and trim.

All things counter, original, spare, strange;
    Whatever is fickle, freckled (who knows how?)
        With swift, slow; sweet, sour; adazzle, dim;
You co-create, whose beauty is past change.
                                            Praise, God!

KABIR

THE SECRET WORD

O how may I ever express that secret word, O God?
O how can I say You are not like this, and You are like that?
If I say that You are within me, the universe is ashamed;
If I say that You are without me, it is falsehood.
You make the inner and the outer worlds to be indivisibly one.
Where are the words to tell truly who You are?

WHO ARE YOU?

We rejoice, O God, that:
You are in us, and we are in You,
Each being distinct, yet ever united.

You are the tree, the seed, and the cell;
You are the flower, the fruit, and the shade;
You are the sun, the light, and the lighted;
You are the manifold form of infinite space;
You are the breath, the word, and the meaning;
You are the limit and the limitless.
You are the Immanent Mind in us;
You are the Supreme Soul within the soul.

Blessed are all who see You.

TOYOHIKO KAGAWA

TEACH ME

O God, teach me how to dispense with unnecessary things.

WHERE YOU DWELL

We are mindful, O God, that You dwell among the lowliest people of the Earth, that You sit on the dust-heap among those in the slums and those in prison, that you are present with the juvenile delinquents and the homeless, that You throng with the beggars seeking bread, that You suffer with the sick, and that You stand in line with the unemployed. May we be mindful that when we forget the unemployed, we forget You.

KENYAN PRAYER

DELIVER ME!

From the cowardice that dare not face new truth,
From the laziness that is content with half truth,
From the arrogance that thinks it knows all truth:
    Good God, deliver me!

JOHANNES KEPLER

AN ASTRONOMER'S PRAYER

I thank You, my Creator, that You have given me joys in Your creation and ecstasy over the work of Your hands.

I have known the glory of Your works as far as my finite spirit was able to comprehend Your infinity.

If have said anything wholly unworthy of You, or have aspired after my own glory, graciously forgive me.

SÖREN KIERKEGAARD

FOR INWARD PEACE

Calm the waves of this heart, O God; calm its tempests.
Calm yourself, O my soul, so that God is able to rest in you, so that God's peace may cover you.
Yes, You can give us peace, O God, peace that the whole world can never take away.

CONFIDENCE IN YOU

Dear Deathless Power in each atom, amoeba, and galaxy;
And also within each teacher, parent, and child:
Our thought is turned toward You
As we seek You with the sureness of a homeward bound bird.

Our confidence in You would be no momentary leap,
No unproductive birth pangs nor waterless clouds;
But from the fullness of our hearts, our hopes arise toward You,
Quenching our thirst and giving life's noblest satisfaction.

UNCHANGEABLE

Dear God who is unchangeable, unchangeable in love:
May we submit ourselves to the discipline of Your unchangeable-
ness
Through our unconditional love of You,
Whereby we find rest and remain at rest in You.

O God who is unchangeable,
Yet who in infinite love is moved —
Even by the need of a sparrow —
May there be wrought in us through prayer
Such changes as will bring our lives into unity with You,
O God who is unchangeable in love.

THE COURAGE TO HOPE

God, give me once more the courage to hope.
Fertilize my barren mind.
Let me hope again.

YOU HAVE LOVED US FIRST

Great Companion, You have loved us first.
May we never forget that You are love,
So that this sure conviction might triumph in our hearts
Over the whirling of the world,
Over the inquietude of the soul,
Over the anxiety for the future,
Over the fright of the past,
Over the distress of the moment.
May this conviction discipline our soul
So that our hearts might remain faithful and sincere
In the love which we bear to all those we love as ourselves.

YOU HEAR OUR CRY

Great is Your kingdom, O You who bears the weight of the stars and governs the forces of the world.

Numberless are those who have life through You, yet You hear the cry of all creatures. You hear the cry of all without confusing their voices and without playing favorites. You hear not only the voice of one who is responsible for many others. You hear not only the voice of one who prays for dear ones. No, You also hear the most miserable, the most abandoned, the most solitary person — in the desert, in the multitude.

If the forgotten one has become unknown in the crowd, having ceased to be anything more than a number on a list, You remember the person and the name. If in the thick shadows of dread, in the prey of terrible thoughts, we are abandoned, abandoned almost by the language we speak, still You would not have forgotten us. You would understand our language, You who hears the cry of all. You find a way to us which is prompter than light and more constant than the stars.

TO WILL ONE THING

Holy One, what is a person without You? What is all that we know, vast accumulation though it be, but a chipped fragment if we do not know You? What is all our striving but a half-finished work if we do not know You, You who are one and all.

Give us the wisdom to know one thing, to know You: the heart to receive this understanding, and the will to will only one thing. In prosperity, may we have perseverance to will one thing; amidst distractions, may we concentrate to will one thing; and in suffering , may we have the patience to will one thing.

God of the beginning and the end: at the dawn of day, give to the young the resolution to will one thing; and as the day wanes, give to the old renewed remembrance of the first resolution that the first may be like the last and the last like the first, in possession of a life that has willed one thing. May we from the beginning to the end of our lives will one thing: to know and to love You who are one and all.

WORKS OF LOVE

How could anything rightly be said about love if You were forgotten, O God,
You from whom all love comes;
You who holds back nothing but gives Yourself in love;
You who are love, so the lovers are only what they are through being in You?
How could anything rightly be said about love if You were forgotten,
You who manifests what love is,

You who reminds us to love as we are loved;
You who are everywhere present and never without the works of love,
   the acts of love?
How could anything rightly be said about love if You were forgotten, O
   Love Eternal?

YOU ARE NEAR

   We know that You are present everywhere, O God. You are near
should anyone call upon You at this moment from a bed of sickness, or
cry out to You in greater need upon the seas. You are also near in Your
houses where people gather to praise You; some perhaps flying from
heavy thoughts or followed by heavy thoughts, but some coming from a
quiet life of daily contentment—yet all are drawn to seek You, the Friend
of the thankful; the Consolation of the weak; the Refuge of the anxious;
the Confidante of the afflicted as You count their tears; the Comfort of the
dying. May You be found with Your gift for everyone who needs it.

D. H. LAWRENCE

PAX

All that matters is to be at one with You, the living God;
to be a creature in Your house, O God of Life!
Like a cat asleep on a chair
at peace, in peace
at home, at home in the house of the living,
sleeping on the hearth, and yawning before the fire.

Sleeping on the hearth of the living world,
yawning at home before the fire of life
feeling the presence of You, the living God
like a great reassurance
a deep calm in the heart
a presence
as of a master, a mistress sitting on the board
in their own and greater being,
in the house of life.

ABRAHAM LINCOLN

MIGHT

God, give us faith that right makes might.

GEORGE MacRAE

THE HOPE OF TOMORROW

O God, the alpha and the omega,
      the first and the last,
      the beginning and the end,
   grace with Your presence
all our endings and our beginnings.

Give us joy in the newness of life,
    humility in the moment of our accomplishment,
    gratitude for all that we have been given.

You who now are,
      and who was
      and who is to come,
   be ever present in our transitions.

Lift our hearts beyond the satisfactions of the moment
      to the needs of the times,
   and sanctify our now
      with the memory of our then
      and the promise and hope of Your tomorrow.

PETER MARSHALL

PEACE WITHOUT PAIN

God, have pity upon us.
We want peace without pain and security without sacrifice.
We want peace but not the perils of peacemaking.
O God, may we learn what love is.

SUCCESS

God, give us the grace to take things as they are
And to make them what they ought to be.

FOR WORLD NEIGHBORLINESS

O God, we pray for a broader vision of the needs of humanity, and a deeper compassion to fill those needs; for a planting of the seeds of concern for all humanity in our hearts; for a tapping of the wells of generosity.

May we live together as people who have been forgiven a great debt.

May we be gentle, walking softly with one another.

May we be understanding, lest we shall add to the world's sorrow or cause to flow needless tears.

May we be as anxious for the rights of others as we are for our own.

May we be as eager to forgive as we are to seek forgiveness.

May we know no barriers of creed or race or sex, that our love may be like Yours—a love that sees all people as Your children and our kin.

May we be ministers of humanity.

JAMES MARTINEAU

A PRAYER OF CONSECRATION

Eternal God, who commits to us the swift and solemn trust of life: since we know not what a day may bring forth, but only that the hour for serving You is always present, may we wake to Your instant claims, not waiting for tomorrow, but yielding today. Lay to rest the resistance of our passion, indolence, or fear. Consecrate the way our feet may go, and the humblest work will shine, and the roughest faces be made plain. Lift us above unrighteous anger and mistrust into faith and hope and charity, through steady reliance on You. So may we be modest in our time of wealth, patient under disappointment, ready for danger, serene in death. In all things, draw us to Yourself that Your lost image may be traced again, and we may be at one with You.

SIDNEY MEAD

FOR WISDOM

God of all, grant us our due portion of wisdom.

May our minds be set fast on justice; may our hearts be soft with compassion as we daily walk humbly with You, the God of both.

May we be eyes when others cannot see, ears when they cannot hear, hands when their work languishes, and feet when they stumble on the way.

Grant us grace to love our brothers and sisters as they are, for what they can be; and more grace to resist trying to make them over into our image.

EDNA ST. VINCENT MILLAY

GOD'S WORLD

O World, I cannot hold You close enough!
 Your winds, Your wide gray skies!
 Your mists that roll and rise!
Your woods, this autumn day, that ache and sag
And all but cry with color! That giant crag
To crush! To life the lean of that black bluff!
World, World, I cannot get You close enough!

Long have I known a glory in it all,
 But never knew I this;
 Here such a passion is
As stretches me apart. God, I fear
You've made the World too beautiful this year.
My soul is all but out of me—let fall
No burning leaf; prithee, let no bird call.

SAMUEL H. MILLER

FORGIVE ME

Forgive me, God, for prayers my lips too easily speak, for prayers made out of words which are nothing but words. Forgive me for the prayers I borrow from the agony of others without suffering myself, for prayers of light and glory unballasted by the darkness and depth from which such things bloom. Forgive me for prayers unwashed by the silences of mystery. Forgive me, God, for prayers wherein I pampered myself and consecrated my false faith. Forgive me, and teach me how to pray.

MOHAMMED

TO LOVE YOU

O God, grant us to love You;
Grant us to do deeds that win Your love.
May the love of You be dearer to us than wealth,
And dearer even than cool water.

DIANN NEU

BLESSED BE OUR HANDS

Blessed be the work of our hands.

Blessed be these hands that touch life.
Blessed be these hands that nurture creativity.
Blessed be these hands that hold pain.
Blessed be these hands that embrace with passion.
Blessed be these hands that tend gardens.
Blessed bed these hands that close in anger.
Blessed be these hands that plant new seeds.
Blessed be these hands that harvest ripe fields.
Blessed be these hands that clean, wash, mop, scrub.
Blessed be these hands that become knotty with age.
Blessed be these hands that wrinkle and scar from doing justice.
Blessed are these hands that reach out and are received.
Blessed are these hands that hold the promise of the future.

Blessed be the works of our hands and hearts.

REINHOLD NIEBUHR

GRACE, COURAGE, WISDOM

God, give us grace to accept with serenity the things that cannot be changed, courage to change the things that should be changed, and wisdom to distinguish the one from the other.

TEACH US

O God, the sovereign of nations, teach us how we may build a common life in which the nations of the world may find peace and justice. Show us what we ought to do. Show us also what are the limits of our power and what we cannot do. Recall us to our dignity as co-workers with You now and evermore.

FOR ALL PEOPLE

O God, we pray for all sorts and conditions of people:
For all who toil in the burden and heat of the day, that they may enjoy the rewards of their industry, that they may not be defrauded of their due, and that we may never cease to be mindful of our debt to them for making our life tolerable;

For those in authority, who have power over others, that they may not use it for selfish advantage but be guided to do justice and to love mercy.

For those who have been worsted in the battles of life, whether by the inhumanity of others, their own limitations, or the fickleness of fortune, that they may contend against injustice without bitterness, and learn how to accept what cannot be altered, with patience;

For the rulers of nations that they may promote peace among the peoples and establish justice in our common life.

For the teachers and ministers of Your power, for artists, scientists and interpreters of the spiritual life, that they may not corrupt the truth to which they are committed;

For prophets and seers who awaken us from our sloth, that they may hold their torches high in a world darkened by prejudice.

O God, who has bound us together in this bundle of life, give us the grace to understand how our lives depend upon one another and our responsibilities to You.

URSULA M. NIEBUHR

FOR THE DAY OF LIGHT

O God, who has placed us in a world You and we constantly create, we give thanks as we work and as we pray. We praise You for the day of light and life, for the night which brings rest and sleep, and for the ordered course of nature, seedtime and harvest. We bless You for the joy of children and the wisdom of the old. We thank You for the love of God and people which shines forth in commonplace lives, and above all for the vision of You in silent meditation, in fellowship, in the sacrament of the shared life, and in prayer. We praise Your name now and forevermore.

ELSE NIEMOELLER

FOR THE WORLD'S CHILDREN

Lover of humanity, who cares for even one sparrow's fall, we thank You that Your infinite eye is upon all the children of the world. Whatever the circumstances, we pray that we may help to release them from the forces that scar: hunger, homelessness, hatred, and lies. Give to each of us some sense of responsibility that all children everywhere may come into their full human heritage.

ORDERS OF WORSHIP
FOR MANCHESTER COLLEGE, OXFORD

FOR OUR COUNTRY

Almighty God, we are thankful for this land which is our home. From shore to shore may we be blessed with honorable industry and sound learning. May we shun needless violence and discord as we act to defend our liberties and preserve our unity. May those to whom the authority of government is entrusted serve with wisdom, prudence, and courage, so that there may be true justice and peace at home and abroad. May the many languages spoken by the people of this nation strengthen us in our common pursuit of happiness. May we and all nations unite in contributing what is excellent both to one another and to You, the deathless Giver and Receiver of our lives.

WE SING PRAISE

Everliving God, we rejoice in Your constancy throughout all change. We sing praise to You for the newness of each morning, as well as for the faithfulness of night.

We rejoice in the riches of nature and in the very fact of our existence today. You raise us above lowness of mind and sadness of spirit by enabling us to see our work and our rest, our joy and our sorrow, as parts of Your divine process.

GEOFFREY S. PAIN

FOR THE GIFTS OF SCIENCE

God of truth and Lover of humanity, we praise You for the gifts of science, which have added to our well-being and delivered us from many agonies of pain. We rejoice in the long roll of scientists who rendered selfless service in the advancement of knowledge, including those who gave life itself in the battle against disease. We pray for the illumination of all who seek the cause and cure of the dangerously declining environment of the planet. Deliver us from the employment of Your gifts in the destruction of reason and life, whether in war or peace, so all the days of our years may contribute to the enhancement of the Earth.

THEODORE PARKER

OUR FATHER AND OUR MOTHER

Creating and Protecting Power, our Father and our Mother, we lift up our psalm of thanksgiving to You. You hold the world in Your arms of love. It sings thanksgiving to You every morning, evening and noon. We praise You for Your blessings. We desire to be deeply conscious of Your presence, which fills all time, which occupies all space. We would know You as You are.

We thank You for the happiness that attends us in our daily life, for the joys of our daily work, for the success which You give to the labor of our hands. We thank You for the plain and common household joys of life, for the satisfactions of friendship, for the blessedness of love in all the dear relationships of life.

We thank You that amid hopes that so often deceive us, amid expectations that fail and perish, we have still our faith in You. In our sorrow and sadness we look up to You, and when mortal friends fail us, and the urn that held our treasured joys is broken into fragments, and the wine of life is scattered at our feet, O God, we rejoice to know that You understand our lot. We thank You that You hold each one of us, yes, all Your children and the universe itself, as a mother folds her baby to her bosom.

THE HIGHER GOOD

Dear God, I will not ask for wealth or fame,
Though once they would have joyed my carnal sense;
I shudder not to bear a hated name,
Wanting all wealth, myself my sole defense,
But give me, God, eyes to behold the truth,
A seeing sense that knows the eternal right;
A heart with pity filled and gentlest ruth;
A robust faith that makes all darkness light;
Give me power to labor for humankind;
Make me the mouth of such as cannot speak;
Eyes let me be to the groping and the blind;
A conscience to the base; and to the weak,
Let me be hands and feet; and to the foolish, mind;
And lead still farther on such as Your kingdom seek.

FATHER AND MOTHER OF ALL

Eternal One, I bathe my soul in Your infinity.

Transcendent God! Yet, ever immanent in all that is, I flee to You, and seek repose and soothing in my Mother's breast. From all this dusty world, You will not lose a molecule of earth or spark of light. Father and Mother of all things that are, I flee to You, and in Your arms find rest; My God! I thank You for Your love.

OPEN OUR INNER EYES

Eternal One whose presence fills all space and occupies all time, who has a dwelling-place in every humble heart that trusts in You: we bless Your for Your loving-kindness, knowing that You love us better even than the mothers who have borne us. We thank You this day for the broad great world beneath our feet, for these wondrous heavens above our heads which mightily You sow with starry seeds; for the rivers as they roll and the ocean as it ebbs and floods. O God, they tell us of Your power; they talk of Your wisdom; they charm us with tidings of Your love.

A greater revelation is Your still small voice, which whispers in our soul that all this magnificence is but a drop of You, a little sparklet that has fallen from Your presence, O Central Fire and Radiant Light of all. The outward things are but a whisper of Your wisdom.

O God, open our inner eyes that we may see You as You are and serve You with our daily life. Arm us for the duty which You give us to do, every day's work in its own day. May duty be supreme over desire and our daily life be beautiful, one continual sacrament to You.

INFINITE MOTHER, INFINITE FATHER

Infinite Mother, the parent of our bodies and our souls: We know You always have us in Your care and that You cradle the world beneath Your eye; we would be conscious of Your presence with us.

Infinite Father, we thank You for this great human world added to this earth and air and sea. We thank You for the mighty capacities You have given us for thought and toil, for beauty and for duty. We thank You for this soul of ours whereby we know You, our Father and our Mother, and have serene delight in Your continual presence and Your love. We thank You that when we wander from Your ways, Your love forsakes us not but reaches out to bring the wanderer back home wiser and better. We thank You that we may live noble lives, that we may become whole.

OUR DAILY LIVES

Infinite Presence who lives and move and has Your being in all that is above us and around us and underneath us: we remember that it is in You that we also live and move and have our being. Conscious of Your presence, we would look on our daily lives, that the murmur of our business, the roar of the street and the jar of the noisy world, may mingle in the prayer of our aspiration and hymn of gratitude. May the meditations of our hearts draw us nearer to You, always above us and about us and within.

When we are weak and poor and foolish, may we remember the Source of all strength and all wisdom and all riches; and when we grow strong and rich, wise and good, may we never forget our duty to the poor, the weak, the foolish, but love others as we love ourselves.

We pray that in every emergency of our lives, we may be faithful to the duty which the day demands , doing what must be done, bearing what must be borne, and so growing greater from our toil and our sufferings, till we transfigure ourselves into noble images of humanity.

YOU BIND TOGETHER THE AGES

Living God who fills the world and yet is not far from any one of us, we would join ourselves to You, and warm and freshen our spirit in the sunlight of Your countenance, and come away strengthened and made whole.

We thank Your for the little children, whose coming foretells that progress kingdom of righteousness which is ever at our doors, waiting to be revealed; giving joy to many a father's and mother's heart.

We thank You for the power of youth, for its green promise, its glad foretelling, and its abundant hope. We thank You for the strength of manhood and womanhood, into whose hands You commit the family, the community, the nation and the world.

We bless You for the old age which crowns the head with silver honors, the fruit of long and experienced life, and enriches the ear with wisdom which babyhood knew not, which Youth could not comprehend, and only long-continued maturity could make perfect.

O God, we thank You that You bind together the ages of infancy and Youth, adulthood and old age by the sweet ties of family and social love.

Almighty Power, All-knowing Wisdom, we thank You for Yourself and for Your arms around this dusty world.

THANK YOU

Perpetual Presence, always near to us, may the fire of our gratitude be kindled and our souls flame up towards You.

We thank You for the world of matter under our feet, over our head, and about us on every side.

We thank You for the bread we eat, for the garments we put on, for the houses which hold us, for the sleep which all night slides into our bones, bringing strength to the weary and health to the sick.

We thank You for the vast gifts which You have bestowed upon us, for these bodies so wonderfully made, for the ever-questioning mind which hungers for truth and beauty, for the vision of You held by Your children of every age and every land.

We thank You for great philosophers and prophets and poets who have gathered justice and taught love as well as for the billions of unremembered men and women who in their common callings were faithful to the light which shone upon them, and we rejoice in the heritage which their toil has won and bequeathed to us.

O God, our Father and our Mother, may we know You as You are, for Yours is the kingdom and the power and the glory forever and ever.

TO JOIN THE HUMAN RACE

O God, may we join the human race in daring to live in the prophetic spirit: seeking inspiration like the seers and sages of this and other lands, judging the past as they, acting on the present like them, envisioning a new and nobler era of the spirit.

May our doctrines and forms fit the soul as the limbs fit the body: growing out of it, growing with it.

May we have communities for the whole person: truth for the mind, good works for the hands, love for the heart; and for the soul that aspiring after perfection, that unfaltering faith in life, which like lightning in the clouds, shines brightest when elsewhere it is most dark.

FRANCIS GREENWOOD PEABODY

FOR A SENSE OF PROPORTION

Amid the confusing multiplicity of our desires, we pray for a finer sense of proportion in the judgement of our problems and our plans. A multitude of details hide our view of the larger purposes of life; misunderstandings cloud the day with foolish animosity; we cherish our grievances and waste our friendships; we see things not as they are but as we wish them to be.

Deliver us from these sins of disproportion, that our small concerns may not hide from view the light of Your eternal power and that anxiety about trifles may be conquered by our commitment to the True and Beautiful and Good. Show us the excellence in others which we have failed to see. Turn us from our own needs to the larger world of public affairs. Save us from narrow and provincial views. Restore to us a fresh sense of proportion, so the incidental may not hide the eternal or the vexing problems of the day not destroy our own peace of mind.

COURAGE

O God, we are grateful for the great adventure of living. We pray not for immunity from risks but for courage to face them. We pray not to be saved out of the world but to ally ourselves with the saviors of the world. Give us courage to face facts without evasion or self-deception. Give us strength, amidst the perplexities of life, that we may experience the exhilaration of constructive conflict and the joy of victory. Arm us for the campaign of life with unperturbed faith, unconquered hope, and the tranquil courage born of love.

FOR A QUIET MIND

Wearied by the haste and waste of the day, we turn to You, the Source of our peace and strength, and pray for the gift of a quiet mind. Transient troubles of the day crowd upon us; we are provoked to irritating words; petty decisions disquiet our temper and dissipate our strength. Lift us up from this slough of despond to firm ground, that duty may be rescued from perplexity and work be unsevered from tranquility. We do not pray that life be less demanding but only that we may not lose poise, and that, in the events of each passing day, we may serve You with a quiet mind.

LESLIE T. PENNINGTON

TRIUMPHANT FAITH

Almighty God, to whom people in all varieties of living faiths lift up their hearts, from the depths of our need and in the greatness of hope, we lift up our hearts.

We would see beyond the differences, the unity of Your all-pervading light. We would be humble before those differences which divide us from the seamless mantle of Your united power. We would be patient with the impatient and gentle with the pride of the humiliated and the arrogance of those who are afraid, knowing that gentleness and patience are made possible by the certainty of a triumphant faith.

Through all the perils of our times, we would not be content to hold the spiritual citadels of yesterday. We would dare to move forward with searching minds and probing hearts, knowing that life will ever answer our highest endeavor and will reveal to us the duties which arise from new occasions, the opportunities which lie hidden in new relationships, the joys of fresh creative labors, and the peace of spirits which dare to rise in living trust to You. In the hour of failure sustain, us with the vision of what yet may be; and in the hour of triumph, chasten us with the consciousness of unfinished work.

FOR QUIET STRENGTH

For persons with clear and steady minds, for valiant spirits untouched by pretense, jealousy of rancor, we lift our hearts in joy to You, O God. In them we know the certain touch and freshness of Your creation.

Amid the drift of blind confusion, we would be quiet, sure and true. Amid the whispering winds of fear, the gathering tides of mistrust, the storms of hysteria, the undertows of doubt, we seek the steady poise of Your perspective. When darkness settles over the earth, we seek Your inner light. Before blank walls of impotence, we seek the hidden pass which opens widening vistas of Your new creation. Amid the lonely crowd, we dare the way of simple friendliness, of clear-felt truth and clear-spoken word until the minds and hearts of folk in every circumstance and place shall know the quiet strength and peace and joy of souls full-wakened to Your beauty, majesty and power.

FILL OUR LIVES

God of Tranquility at the heart of endless agitation, dynamic Power in perfect repose: we turn to You knowing that You will ever meet those who truly seek You with their whole heart, giving them light in their darkness, strength and skill and fortitude in their labor, patience in adversity, and Your deep peace in their hearts.

We now yield our spirits to Your spirit, that we may quietly release ourselves from anxiety, that we may honestly and resolutely face the weakness and mistakes of our lives, that we may relax our troubled souls in the certainty of Your perpetual presence and peace.

May the fullness of Your spirit fill our lives, as the incoming tide fills every inlet of the shore, as the rising sun floods the earth with light, as the freshening wind stirs the leaves of the forest.

THE MEASURELESS RESOURCE

God of our fathers and mothers, may we be worthy of the heritage which is upon us. Confirm within us the memories and influences of our growing years: the light which shines in our darkness, the insights which stirred and awakened our hearts, the sowing of winged seeds which bear within us the flower and fruit of the future.

Enable us to find, amid the beauty and terror of existence, the paths which lead to Your everlasting light and strength, grace and peace. Open our eyes to the vision of Your measureless resource. Open our minds to the creative order of Your law. Open our hearts to the silent beauty of Your grace. Nerve our wills with the quiet majesty of Your power.

May we remember always that we are not alone, that Your spirit moves within our minds purifying, strengthening, exalting, and uniting our lives through Your power, which no division can sunder and no evil resist. Make us worthy to share in some small measure this movement of Your light upon the darkness, Your love upon hate, and the order of Your life upon the forces of evil, chaos, death.

WE ARE NOT ALONE

In the felt sense of Your presence, O God, we know that we are not alone; that when we are seeking truth most bravely, we are least alone. A mighty gathering of witnesses is about us: the remembered spirits of our beloved and honored dead; the hosts of our living companions upon the way; the host of each new generation — the unborn children of tomorrow and tomorrow and tomorrow, bearing with them the fresh promise of Your ever-new creation to the last syllable of unrecorded time.

Within the life of this great company, grant us some vision, O God; even some momentary vision of a life of possibilities which make our ordinary life seem but a foretaste of what may be. Grant us the quiet patience and endurance to follow on through hours of darkness as through hours of light, guided by that vision of what we have seen, until more and more our whole world is transfigured in Your Light.

WE FIND OURSELVES

Mysterious Power in which our lives are set and of which our world is made: in wonder, gratitude and awe, we turn to You. We confess that no human mind can fully comprehend You, and that no human heart can fully sound the creative depths of Your creative power. We confess that we are restless parts of Your embracing wholeness — fragments of Your eternal mind, Your eternal spirit— forever restless until we lose ourselves and find ourselves in You. Within the eternal freshness of Your creation, we seek fulfillment of more abundant life — not for ourselves alone but for one another, for all Your children of every nation, race and creed. As stars upon their trackless way, as homing birds upon their certain flight — in storm and in sunshine, in darkness as in light — so we would set our course by You. We would find in You: the life and motion of our souls, our freedom, our everlasting home and our enduring peace.

WE ASK NOT

O God, we ask not that our way shall be easy, but that we shall have strength of heart to walk its uttermost mile.

We ask not that our burden shall be light, but that we shall bear it with gallant and undaunted spirits.

We ask not that we, or those we love, shall be spared the suffering and loss of all who bear the brunt of life's battle, but that we and they shall win — even through strife — a nobler fellowship, a sounder sense of right, a more august and creative sense of living in which even our dead shall be fulfilled, even this suffering and sorrow be gathered into greater beauty, life and peace.

THE GIFT OF LIFE

Source of Life implanted in each one of us, true Master of destiny, Guardian of the unknown, the unexplored, the unfulfilled: we turn to You as mariners upon the unknown deep, trusting alike the inner powers of life and the elements in which we live and move and have our being.

We thank You for the gift of life itself, its mystery and unfolding power:
> for gifts of mind to trace the hidden order of Your law,
> for gifts of heart to find the beauty of Your grace in nature,
> for gifts of skill to know, in our creative work, Your joy in all creation.

We would be humble before the wonder of Your unfolding creation:
> of life, of healing, of life's transfigurations;
> of time and time's fulfillment;
> of that imperishable beauty which outlasts time.

We would deal tenderly with the divine potentialities of every living thing, of Your life within ourselves, as in all those we meet upon life's way.

Make us divinely sensitive to our finest hidden potentialities that in their fulfillment we may share in Your creative work of healing and love.

May Yours be the glory forever.

MORNING

We lift our eyes to the everlasting hills of light;
We drink from the everlasting springs of life;
We know once more the freshness of the morning;
We find You in the life and motion of our souls.

PLATO

A PRAYER OF SOCRATES

Give me beauty in the inward soul; and may the outward and the inward be at one. May I reckon the wise to be the wealthy, and may I have such a quantity of gold as a temperate person, and only a temperate person, can carry.

VIVIAN T. POMEROY

PRAYER OF THANKSGIVING

God of All Life, we thank You for our lives and for all they hold of happiness and work and play.

We thank You for the morning and evening skies of a land where citizens can speak out.We thank You for friendship, for those who look kindly upon us even when we fail, and who help to bring us back to our bravest selves again.

We thank You for the encouragements of success, for the disciplines of failure, for the spurs of dissatisfaction, and for the creative spirit which can arise from defeat.

We thank You for the healing strength of laughter, for the gentle play of wit, and for rare splendid moments.

We thank You for prized books and music and pictures, which move the heart; for letters from those we love; and for the song long remembered.

We thank You for the freedom which growing older each day gives us, so that we have more big things to care about, and fewer little things about which to cry.

We thank You for common joys of all kinds — the walking to sunlight through the window, the good smell of the earth on rainy days, the gift of sleep after tiring work or sport.

God of All Life, we thank You for this undaunted human life of ours; may we live ever to Your glory.

REJOICE

God of fire and water, joy and sorrow: as we celebrate life, we rejoice in the wonder of being loved, the fidelity of friends, and the glad surprise of being forgiven. We are grateful for the strength to forget what is not worth remembering and for the power to remember what becomes more precious as the years go on.

THE ELIXIR

God of the wind and sand, sun and moon, joy and beauty, loneliness and sorrow:

We thank You for the magic in our human lives often turning our drabness into gold.

We thank You for the wonder of being loved;

for the fidelity of friends;

for the glad surprise of being forgiven;

for the strength to forget what is not worth remembering;

for the power to remember things which become more precious as the years go on;

for the discovery that in the darkness there are presences which are hidden from us by the light.

Touch into living flame again the hearts which have grown weary with the weight of things; and when duty tires, grant us the love which goes gladly all the way.

I WILL LOOK UP

Deathless Light of the World, may this day fill up all its blue in our hearts, whatever it may bring to our skies. May we live it as those for whom all the yesterdays mark some better way than leads to dusty death. May we march with a song; may our feet be shod with a fine hard faith in living; and may we win at least some little token of the eternal from the fleeting hours.

We bless You for the work we have to do, and for our measure of health with which to do it; and for the spirit's assurance that even by the weakest, there is always something to be done. If doing without must be our portion, may we accept it with the valor of a decisive act.

We bless You for the hopes which struggle out of our most wretched failures; for the chagrin which disturbs our shallow successes; and for the secret laughter which is somewhere in our bitterest tears.

We bless You for the constant love of those with whom we dwell; for the friends who remain faithful even in their woundings; and for the surprising kindness we often meet from strangers.

We bless You for those before us who sacrificed to benefit us, and for the host of chivalry, beyond number or name, whereby the giving has never ceased and never shall.

O True Light of Life, we lift this day to You.

THE MOMENT

O God, our home and also our long way; our rest and our ongoing courage; our haven and our saving hope, we praise You for this mortal life.

We praise You for the flow of time on which all things pass;

We praise You for the spirit in us greater than the flowing tide;

We praise You that there are grand moments better than a thousand days;

We praise You that in the greatness of life, the hearts of young and old come very close together, and even the distant ones come back.

We praise You that in high moments, when hearts are full, there is Someone to praise.

HEALING AFTER PAIN

O God our undying hope, we thank You for the warmth which steals back into our hearts after a while;

for the healing which comes to wounded bodies and spirits through time;

for the blessed fact that the flood of pain does not last forever and for the incredible bliss when the tide begins to ebb;

for the cheerfulness which breaks into our dark dungeon and strikes off our fetters when least expected, we know not how;

for the strange sadness which haunts our brightest hours because our hearts are made for a joy deeper than happiness;

for the insurgent courage which lifts its head above past mistakes and worse, and affirms its right to try again;

for the golden thread of valor and good will never quite lost in the tragic wanderings of men and nations;

for the labors of those who have sown that others may reap;

for the dear kindness of those who see us as we once were.

We thank You, God of our little faith, our greater hope, and above all our faltering love, which can never fail because it is more Yours than ours.

WEEK PAST AND WEEK BEGINNING

O God, we bring before You at this hour the life we have lived in the week that is past.

We thank You for everything we were able to do and found good in the doing.

We thank You for duties which were not so welcome when they appeared, but left us glad that we had done them.

We thank You for the friends we knew we could trust; for persons who made us glad to have met them; and for all the workers who maintained the fabric of the world.

We thank You for little victories won over ourselves; for all the words well spoken, and for things wisely left unsaid.

O God, we bring before You at this hour the week now beginning, and our hopes for it.

If there are things left undone which reproach us, may we have a steadfast mind to do them.

If there are things we ought to finish, may we turn to them again.

But may we not be downcast because there are some things we shall never finish, inasmuch as they are so great.

May we not become slothful because time is long; may we not become feverish because time is short.

May the past be our benediction, and the future be our challenge.

May we lift up our strength to greet each day, and may Your song be with us in the night.

FROM THE HEART

O God, we thank You for life, and for all it holds of happiness and work and play and risk and courage and beauty.

We thank You for all the adventures of the mind whereby we pursue what is true, grapple with difficult problems, and share a little in the vast heritage of man's knowledge.

We thank You for the firmness of reasonable people in refusing to follow extremists; but we also thank You for the pioneers of advancing thought in science, art, and religion.

We thank You for all heroic souls who shame our cowardice; for all sympathetic souls who communicate encouragement; for all human souls, seldom wearing haloes, who kindle our desire to be really good.

We thank You for friendship and the faces of those who, when we fail, help to bring us back to our bravest selves again.

We thank You for the exchange of gifts, for letters to and from those we love, for the sparkle of a pleasant wit, for the refreshment of unforced laughter, and for the song remembered for the singer's sake.

Above all, we thank You for Your call to be ourselves at our best, without miserably trying to be somebody else. So may we grow in the strength to make the best of things, trusting You that they will make the best of us.

RAMANUJA

YOU

You are my Mother and my Father;
You are my Friend and my Teacher;
You are my Wisdom and my Riches;
You are all to me, O God of all Gods.

WALTER RAUSCHENBUSCH

FOR OUR WORLD, OUR EARTH

O God, we thank You for this universe, our great home; for the vastness and richness of our cosmic environment; for the manifoldness of life on the planet of which we are a part.

We are thankful for the morning sun and the clouds and the constellations of stars.

We rejoice in the salt sea and the deep waters and green leaves of grass.

We thank You for our sense by which we experience earth's splendor.

We would have souls open to all this joy, souls saved from being so weighted with care that we pass unseeing when the thornbush by the wayside is aflame with beauty.

Enlarge within us a sense of fellowship with all that lives and moves and has being in space and time, especially with all who share this earth as their common home with us.

Remembering with shame that in the past, we human beings have all too often exercised high dominion with ruthless cruelty, we admit that the voice of the earth, which should have gone up to You in song, has been a groan of travail.

May we so live that our world may not be ravished by our greed nor spoiled by our ignorance.

May we hand on earth's common heritage of life, undiminished in joy when our bodies return in peace to You, our Great Mother who has nourished them.

EVENING PRAYER

O God, we praise You for the night and for sleep. Release our limbs of toil. Smooth our brow of care. Grant us a refreshing draught of forgetfulness. Comfort those who toss on a bed of pain, or whose nerves crave sleep and find it not. Save them from despondent thoughts in the darkness. May they learn to lean on Your all-pervading life and love so, their souls may grow tranquil and their bodies may rest.

WALLACE W. ROBBINS

FOR HOPE AND GOOD CHEER

O God, who has given us the gift of courage so that we may endure hardness and meet danger with a resolute will, grant us Your spiritual benediction that we may have hope to carry us through frustration with good cheer and through defeats with an unrelenting faith in the ultimate victory of Your purpose.

FOR REALITY

O God, who hates illusion and loves reality: grant us a strong grasp of facts and a fair vision of truth; that neither the frights of pain nor the baits of false hopes may misdirect us, nor may we be kept from seeking You with a brave heart.

RUSSIAN PRAYER, 19th CENTURY

FOR OUR FRIENDS THE ANIMALS

Hear our prayer, O God, for our friends, the animals, especially for those animals that are suffering; for all that are overworked and under-fed and cruelly treated; for creations in captivity that bent against the bars; for any that are lost of deserted; for all that are in pain of dying; for all that must be put to death. May those who deal with them have hearts of compassion and gentle hands.

CARL SANDBURG

PRAYERS OF STEEL

Lay me on an anvil, O God.
Beat me and hammer me into a crowbar.
Let me pry loose old walls.
Let me lift and loosen old foundations.

Lay me on an anvil, O God,
Beat me and hammer me into a steel spike.
Drive me into the girders that hold a skyscraper together.
Take red-hot rivets and fasten me to the central girders.
Let me be the great nail holding a skyscraper through blue
        nights into white stars.

LEW SARETT

WIND IN THE PINE

Oh, I can hear you, God, above the cry
    Of the tossing trees—
Rolling your windy tides across the sky,
       And splashing your silver seas
        Over the pine,
        To the water-line
        Of the moon.

    Oh, I can hear you, God,
  Above the wail of the lonely loon—
When the pine-tops pitch and nod—
    Chanting your melodies

Of ghostly waterfalls and avalanches,,
Washing your wind among the branches
   To make them pure and white.

Wash over me, God, with your piney breeze,
   And your moon's wet-silver pool;
Wash over me, God, with your wind and night,
   And leave me clean and cool.

MAY SARTON

PRAYER BEFORE WORK

Great one, austere,
By whose intent the distant star
Holds its course clear,
Now make this spirit soar—
Give it that ease.

Out of the absolute
Abstracted grief, comfortless, mute,
Sound the clear note,
Pure, piercing as the flute:
Give it precision.

Austere, great one,
By whose grace the unalterable song
May still be wrested from
The corrupt lung:
Give it strict form.

A PRAYER

Help us to be the always hopeful
gardeners of the spirit
who know that without darkness
nothing comes to birth
as without light
nothing flowers.

SARUM PRIMER

God be in my head,
>   And in my understanding;

God be in my eyes
>   And in my looking;

God be in my mouth
>   And in my speaking;

God be in my heart
>   And in my thinking;

God be at my end,
>   And at my departing.

WILLIAM SCARLETT

FOR DEMOCRACY

Maker of the stars and Master of the nations of
the earth, we pray for the future of all countries engaged
in the audacious, ever changing, ever challenging experiment
of democracy.. May we never grow weary of out task because
of its difficulties. Grant us faith in humanity and confidence
that truth will triumph in free and open encounter. We seek
flexibility of mind and a willingness to try new experiments, so
that we may create the conditions which make us free and
equal, enhance human dignity and self-resect, and establish a
fair measure of economic security for our people. Bind upon
each of us a sense of our individual accountability to You, that
we may do what is just, rising above prejudice to make the good
of all our aim. So shall we take our place with those who labor
that government of the people, by the people, for the people shall
not perish from the earth, but will express the living common faith
of the human family.

ALBERT SCHWEITZER

FOR ANIMALS

We pray today, O God, for our friends, the animals, especially for animals who are suffering; for animals that are over-worked, under-fed, and cruelly treated; for all wistful creatures in captivity that beat their wings against bars; for any that are lost or deserted or hungry; for all that must be put to death. We pray for them all; and for those who deal with them, we hope for a heart of compassion, gentle hands, and kindly words. We would be true friends to animals.

SENECA

WE ADORE YOU

We adore You, Framer of the Universe; Governor, Disposer, Keeper; You on whom all things depend; Mind of the world; You from whom all things spring; You by whose spirit we live; the Divine Spirit diffused through all; God supremely powerful, always present, above all other powers: we adore you.

SIOUX INDIAN PRAYERS

GREAT SPIRIT

Great Spirit,
The star nations all over the heavens are Yours,
And Yours are the grasses of the earth.
You are older than all need,
Older than all pain and prayer.

Great Spirit,
Teach us to walk the soft earth as relatives to all that live.

I NEED YOUR STRENGTH

Great Spirit, whose voice I hear in the winds and whose breath gives life to the whole world, I come before You as one of Your many children.

Grant me to walk in beauty and that my eyes may ever behold the crimson sunset.

May my hands treat with respect the things which You have created.

May my ears hear Your voice.

Make me wise that I may understand what You have hidden in every leaf and every rock.

I long for strength not to conquer others but to conquer myself.

May I ever come to You with pure hands and candid eyes, so that my spirit, when life disappears like the setting sun, may stand unashamed before You.

SOCRATES

INWARD BEAUTY

Give me beauty in the inward soul,
And may the inward and the outer be at one.
May I reckon wisdom to be wealth,
And may I have so much gold as a temperate person,
And only a temperate person,
Can bear and carry.

WILLARD L. SPERRY

FORGIVE US

O God, forgive our wanton waste of the wealth of the soil and sea and air; our desecration of natural beauty; our heedlessness of those who shall come after us, if only we be served; our undue love of money; our contempt for small things and our worship of what is big; our neglect of struggling peoples, For such wrongs to our natural and human heritage, and for many things left undone, forgive us, O God.

FOR THE UNCONQUERABLE MIND

We give You thanks, O God, for the harvest of knowledge, patiently gathered over long years by ongoing generations of scholars, and now laid up for the needs of humanity in our universities. For the increasing mastery of special skills, for victory over ills which people have suffered through ignorance, for confidence in the reliable order of nature, for the wisdom which long experience adds to much learning, for ever new light falling on old mysteries, as for all the joys of our part and portion in the unconquerable mind: we give thanks.

COURAGE TO LIVE

Grant, O God, to Your people more courage to live for You. Guard us from rashness, and deliver us from fear. Teach us when by patience we may serve You best, and when by impatience.

STARHAWK

INVOCATION

Nameless One—of many names
Eternal—and ever-changing One
Who is found nowhere—but appears everywhere
Beyond—and within all.

Timeless—circles of the seasons,
Unknowable mystery—known by all.
Lord of the Dance—Mother of all life:

> Be radiant with us,—
> Engulf us with Your love,
> See with our eyes,
> Hear with our ears   ,
> Breathe with our nostrils,
> Touch with our hands,
> Kiss with our lips,
> Open our hearts!

That we may live free at last
Joyful in the single song
Of all that is, was, or ever shall be!

DOUGLAS STEERE

INTO THE CENTER

O God, draw us from the circumference of life, where we have been living, into the Center. Draw us from preoccupation with ourselves into Your presence. Draw us from our claimful selves, and give us Yourself. In Your presence, we find simplicity amidst complexity; and compulsive activities yield to a willingness to live with singleness of heart.

MALCOLM R. SUTHERLAND

SPEAK TO MY CONDITION

In these hushed moments in Your presence, O God, speak to my condition.

I bring before You my hidden fears and secret hopes, my personal perplexities and social responsibilities.

There are decisions to be made and problems to be solved.

There are relationships to rebuild and broken friendships to be reestablished.

There are sorrows to relieve and new faith to find.

There are debts to be paid and transgressions to forgive.

There are new ventures to explore, new battles to wage, and new voyages to sail.

I seek the courage, the hope, the strength and the wisdom to live my life worthily in Your sight.

RABINDRANATH TAGORE

QUESTIONS TO GOD

Age after age, O God, You have sent Your messengers into this pitiless world, who have left their word:

"Forgive all. Love all. Cleanse your hearts from the blood-red stains of hatred."

Adorable are they, ever to be remembered; yet from the outer door, I have turned away today—this evil day—with unmeaning salutation.

Have I not seen secret malignance strike down the helpless under the cover of hypocritical might?

Have I not heard the silenced voice of justice weeping in solitude at night's defiant outrages?

Have I not seen in what agony reckless youth, running mad, has vainly shattered its life against insensitive rocks?

Choked is my voice, mute are my songs today, and darkly my world lies imprisoned in a dismal dream;

and I ask You, O God, in tears:

"Have You Yourself forgiven; have even You loved those who are poisoning Your air and blotting out Your light?

TREES

Be still, my heart, these great trees are prayers.

THIS IS MY PRAYER

Give me the supreme courage of love, this is my prayer—the courage to speak, to do, to suffer at Your will, to lleave all things or be left alone. Strengthen me on errands of danger; honor me with pain; and help me climb to that difficult mood which sacrifices daily to You.

Give me the supreme confidence of love—this is my prayer—the confidence that belongs to life in death, to victory in defeat, to the power hidden in the frailest beauty, to that dignity in pain which accepts hurt but disdains to return it.

NOT ALTOGETHER LOST

I know that this life, missing its ripeness in love, is not altogether lost.

I know that the flowers that fade in the dawn, and the streams that strayed in the desert, are not altogether lost.

I know that whatever lags behind, in this life laden with slowness, is not altogether lost.

I know that my dreams that are still unfulfilled, and my melodies still unstruck, are clinging to Your lute-strings, and they are not altogether lost.

DARKNESS AND LIGHT

The lantern which I carry in my hand makes enemy of the darkness of the farther road,

And this wayside becomes a terror to me, where even the flowering tree frowns like a spectre of scowling menace; and the sound of my own steps comes back to me in the echo of muffled suspicion.

Therefore, I pray for Your own morning light, when the far and the near will kiss each other, and life will be one in love.

THE GRASP OF YOUR HAND

Let me not pray to be sheltered from dangers but to be fearless in facing them.

Let me not beg for the stilling of my pain but for the heart to conquer it.

Let me not crave in anxious fear to be saved but hope for the patience to win my freedom.

Grant me that I may not be a coward, feeling Your mercy in my success alone; but let me find the grasp of

Your hand in my failure.

THE FULLNESS OF PEACE

Send me the love which is cool and pure like Your rain that blesses the thirsty earth and fills the homely earthen jars.

Send me the love that would soak down into the center of being, and from there would spread like the unseen sap through the branching tree of life, giving birth to fruits and flowers.

Send me the love that keeps the heart still with the fullness of peace.

THE INFINITY OF YOUR LOVE

Stand before my eyes, and let Your glance touch my songs into a flame.

Stand among Your stars, and let me find kindled in their lights my own fire of worship.

The earth is waiting at the world's wayside.

Stand upon the green mantle she has flung upon Your path, and let me in her grass and meadow flowers spread my own salutation.

Stand in my lonely evening where my heart watches alone; fill her cup of solitude, and let me feel in myself the infinity of Your love.

STRIKE AT THE ROOT

This is my prayer to You, O God—strike, strike at the root of poverty in my heart.

Give me the strength lightly to bear my joys and sorrows.

Give me the strength to make my love fruitful in service.

Give me the strength never to disown the poor or bend my knees before insolent might.

Give me the strength to raise my mind high above daily trifles.

And give me the strength to surrender my strength to Your will with love.

TEARS OF THE EARTH

We rejoice, O God, that the tears of the earth keep her smiles in bloom.

LET MY COUNTRY AWAKE

Where the mind is without fear, and the head is held high;

Where knowledge is free;

Where the world has not been broken up into fragments by narrow domestic walls;

Where words come out from the depth of truth;

Where tireless striving stretches its arms toward perfection;

Where the clear stream of reason has not lost its way into the dreary desert sand of dead habit;

Where the mind is led forward by You into ever-widening thought and action—

Into that haven of freedom, O God, let my country awake.

TERESA OF AVILA

DELIVER US

God, deliver us from sullen saints!

HENRY DAVID THOREAU

HOLD ON

I pray today that I may:
Hold on to what is good,
    even if it is a handful of earth;
Hold on to what I believe,
    even if it is a tree that stands by itself;
Hold on to what I must do,
    even if it is a long journey;
Hold on to life,
    even when it is easier letting go;
Hold on to Your hand,
    even when I have just lost my way.

May I live in each season as it passes:
    Breathe the air,
    Drink the drink,
    Taste the fruit,
And resign myself to the influence of each.

May I be blown by all the winds;
May I open all my pores and bathe in all the tides of Nature,
    in all her streams and oceans, at all seasons.

May I grow green with spring, yellow and ripe with autumn,
Drink of each season's influence as a vial,
    A true panacea of all remedies,
    Mixed for Your special use.

HOWARD THURMAN

I LAY BARE BEFORE YOU

The concern which I lay bare before You today is:
Whatever disaffection there is between me and those who are or have been very close to me—I would seek the root or cause of such disaffection, and with the illumination of Your mind, O God, to understand it.

I give myself to Your scrutiny that, whatever there may be in me that is responsible for what has happened, I will acknowledge.

Where I have wronged or given offense deliberately or without intention, I seek a face-to-face forgiveness.

What I can undo I am willing to try; what I cannot undo, with that I seek to make my peace.

How to do these things, what techniques to use, with what spirit— for these I need and seek Your wisdom and strength, O God.

Whatever disaffection there is between me and those who are or have been very close to me, I lay bare before You.

OUR LITTLE LIVES

Our little lives, our big problems—these we place upon Your altar!
The quietness in Your temple of silence again and again rebuffs us:
For some there is no discipline to hold them steady in the waiting,
And the minds reject the noiseless invasion of Your spirit.
For some there is no will to offer what is central in the thoughts—
The confusion is so manifest, there is no starting place to take hold.
For some the evils of the world tear down all concentrations
And scatter the focus of the high resolves.

The threat of war covers us with heavy shadows,
Making the days big with forebodings—
The nights crowded with frenzied dreams and restless churnings.
We do not know how to do what we know to do.
We do not know how to be what we know to be.

Our little lives, our big problems—these we place upon Your altar!
Brood over our spirits, Creator;

Blow upon whatever dream You have for us,
That there may glow once again upon our hearths
The light from Your altar.
Pour out upon us whatever our spirits need of shock, of life, of release
That we may find strength for these days—
Courage and hope for tomorrow.

In confidence we rest in Your sustaining grace
Which makes possible triumph in defeat, gain in loss, and love in hate.

We rejoice this day to say:
Our little lives, our big problems—these we place upon Your altar!

JACOB TRAPP

MARK OF THE ETERNAL

Grant us to see things that bear the mark of the eternal:
The beauty that lives with loving kindness,
The transmutation of suffering into wisdom and understanding;
The divine impulse given and received.

Give us to cherish life's perishable beauty
That it may be imperishably present with us,
And may we so pass through the things that are fleeting
As to be richer in the things that endure.

GUIDE US

Guide us, True Light;
Quicken us, True Life;
Feed us, True Bread;
That our hunger for You may be fed,
And that we may be led
Into the Way of Peace.

PRIORITIES

Wisdom, be more precious than possessions without end.
Truth, be more sacred than the pleasing of a friend.
Courage, be our strength to gain the distant goal.
Beauty, send cleansing wonders through the soul.

TUKARAM

MY COMPLAINT

Ah, God, the torment of this task that
You have laid on me
To tell the splendor of Your love!

I sing and sing,
Yet all the while the truth evades telling.

No words there are, no words,
To show You as You are!

Ah, God, the torment of this task
To tell the splendor of Your love!

THE UPANISHADS

LEAD ME

From the unreal, lead me to the real.
From darkness, lead me to light.
From death, lead me to immortality.

JONES VERY

THE SILENT

There is a sighing in the wood,
A murmur in the beating wave;
The heart has never understood
To tell in words the thoughts they gave.

Yet oft it feels an answering tone,
When wandering on the lonely shore;
And could the lips its voice make known,
'T would sound as does the ocean's roar.

And oft beneath the wind-swept pine,
Some chord is struck the strain to swell;
Nor sounds nor language can define, —
'Tis not for words or sounds to tell.

'Tis all unheard, Your silent Voice,
Whose goings forth, unknown to all,
Bids bending reed and bird rejoice,
And fills with music Nature's hall.

Now in the speechless human heart
Ir speaks, where'er our feet have trod;
Beyond the lips deceitful art
To tell of You, the Unseen God.

HERBERT F. VETTER

PULLING AND LETTING GO

*The arvcher hits the target patly by pulling, partly by letting go;
the boatman reaches the landing partly by pulling, partly by letting go.*

Before You, O God, I would learn the rhythm of relaxed strength.
I would find my quiet, constant rhythm in society and solitude, work
and play, duty and pleasure—in all of my relations with persons and
with groups. In worship I would find You as the Many-in-One uniting all
these opposites; I would find You whose presence is fullness of joy.

In You do I put my trust, O God. Whether I move against or with the
stream, You are my strength. Through Your constant movement through
life's ebb and flow, day and night, summer and winter, I find the whole-
some rhythm of my own life.

Let there be fused within my spirit the moving waters of upstream-
downstream faith. When swinging upstream, my soul exults in risk and
danger, embracing the uncertainty of new adventure, keeping the fibres
of the mind forever tough. When carried downstream to my destinaation
without a struggle, I would inscribe upon the memory the full security
of trust: In You I am relaxed and reassured partly by pulling, partly by
letting go.

ETERNAL FRIEND

Beloved One,
Whose presence we know each time we breathe,
We rejoice in Your rhythmic power sustaining us each moment.

Eternal One,
Whose strength we experience day and night in the tides of the sea,
We rejoice in the constancy of Your power to ebb and flow.

Embraceable One,
Whose body includes each member of the human family,
We rejoice that each of us is a precious portion of Your power.

All-knowing One,
Whose passion for knowledges is limited only by our freedom,
We rejoice that we, too share the search to know ourselves, our
    world, and You, our Eternal Friend.

A GRACE

Blessed are You, O Bountiful Power,
Who feeds us and gives life to our flesh,
Who fills our hearts with joy and happiness,
And helps us to help others to be whole.

THE PEOPLE'S PRAYER

Eternal Present Power,
Our hope is that in each event today we may
Accept our past,
Anticipate our future, and
Actualize our finest present possibilities.

THE SACRAMENT OF SILENCE

In the silence, O God, You constantly surround our growing life.

We know You in the silence of the healing wound, the muteness of tenderness, the quiet growth within the sleeping child, the unspoken bonds uniting friend and friend, the still intensity of meditation, the soundless splendor of our changing seasons.

We know You in the sacred silence of our bodies: the secret movement of the hidden cells, the noiseless restoration of the tissues' balance, the unheard ebb and flow within each artery and vein.

We know You in the magic silence of our minds: the mystery of memory, retaining after-images of childhood, youth, and later years; the miracle of imagination, whereby we behold our visions of the city unattained; the marvel of attention, when the mind is focused to absorption on some needful task.

We know You in the hidden silence of our hearts: the never uttered depths of love between a man and a woman, a teacher and a student, a parent and a child; the art of being altogether for another; the faith restoring faith that someone else is utterly for you.

We know You in the fateful silences of faith. We know You in the sacrament of silence.

BENEDICTION

May we forever hope in the possibilities of life;
May we forever share the adventures of ideas;
May we know peace through not expecting the impossible;
May we know joy through helping what is possible come true.

WHAT WE BELIEVE

O God, we believe in the wholeness of life, made known though moving power in wind and sea, and as awakening love within the human heart.

We believe in the goodness of life, of new life struggling to be born, of all life yearning for fulfillment.

We believe in human destiny, the opportunity of each to find the meaning of life through joyful empowerment and reverent service.

We believe that beneath the brokenness of tragedy lie seeds of new creation: that tragedy need never be in vain.

TAME MY HEART

Tame my heart, O God.
Trim my illusions.
Subdue these wild desires that lead to nowhere:

The desire to seem much wiser and much better than I am;
The desire to win, win, win, and never lose;
The desire to retreat when life cries for advance.

This is my prayer to You and to myself:
I pray for inward honesty, for disciplines of soul;
I pray that You will shatter my illusions and tame my restless
    heart.

WHEN WE LOVE

What do we love when we love You, O God?
The beauty of bodies moving in space,
The brightness of light so glad to our eyes,
The fragrance of flowers, bread, wine,
The rhythms of time and melodies of song,
Persons we hold in beloved embrace:
These we love when we love You.

We also love an ampler beauty of body-mind Power:
An ever living fire of Light,
An ever open sky of Harmony,
An always moving Earth of fragrance,
The ecstasy of union which is Love itself:
These we love when we love You.

You do ever send as our strength
What space-time can and cannot contain,
What eating and drinking can and cannot increase,
What wise people can and cannot name,
What citizens of Earth can and cannot see:
The perpetual miracle of endless living Power
Which we love when we love You, Most Beloved One.

VON OGDEN VOGT

A PRAYER OF AFFIRMATION

Before You, O God, we freely affirm our faith:
We believe in the goodness of life, realizable in the present world, available to all the people of the earth who seek the masteries of thew spirit in every condition.
We believe in humanity and in the worth of all persons.
We believe in labor, in the opportunity of all to bring forth in their several callings the fruits of useful living, and in the right of each to the just rewards of industry.
We believe in society, in the ordered life of religion and government, of school and home, of the arts and sciences, and we rejoice in our communion with one another and with the common hopes of humanity.

FOR DAILY WORK

O God whose works are wonders of a fair and beautiful earth, we give thanks for the daily work that each of us has to do, and for the part each may have in the good works of the world. We give thanks for the benefits that are spread abroad by the common labors of all.
For those who sow the fields, till the soil, and prepare the food; for all who fashion wood and gather stones and build houses and shelters for all our doings: we are thankful.
For those who weave and sew; for those who buy and sell; for those who make all manner of things needful for human health and comfort: we are thankful.

For those who sing and dance; for those who teach and those who discover the ways of earth and space; for communicators, poets, painters, seers, composers, designers, who show us some of life's highest joys: we are thankful.

For those who are wise in the policies of state for all who promote justice in international life; for prophets who cry shame on social wrong; for all who enlarge our sense of human rights: we are thankful.

O You who has called us to be workers together with You and with each other, we confess that we too seldom remember the many near at hand and afar who have put forth their strength, yet now starve or suffer want. Guide us to know how best to understand our times, to use our talents, and to divide the harvest.

We rejoice in the power of people in their daily toil, that day by day in all parts of the earth we may go forth to our work, helping to maintain the fabric of the world.

HAIL THE LIGHT

This day we hail the light: the light of the sun that casts a glory upon the beautiful earth; the light of the mind that gathers knowledge and seeks a growing wisdom; the light of love that transfigures all our lives. Let us here walk in the light that through all our days we may have fellowship with one another and with You, O God.

FAITH THAT UNITES

We are united in the efforts of faith:
faith in truth, in the growth of knowledge and understanding;
faith in love, in the labors and rewards of friendly living;
faith in people, in our powers to build an earthly commonwealth
    of freedom and of peace;
faith in life, the life of all things that is Your life, O God, whose service
    is perfect freedom, whose presence is fullness of joy.

ACT OF AFFIRMATION

We believe in You, O God, the life of all that is: sovereign in wisdom, goodness and power; and working everywhere for justice and peace and love.

We believe in the ideal of human life which reveals itself as love of You and love of humankind.

We believe in the growth of Your kingdom on earth, and that our loyalty to truth, to righteousness, and to other human beings, is the measure of our desire for its coming.

We believe that the living and the dead are in Your hands, O God, and that underneath both are Your everlasting arms.

WONDROUS POWERS

We rejoice this day in the wondrous powers of earth and sky that sustain us: the fallow soils, the sun and rain that quicken seeds and flowers, the ripening grains that grow unto the harvest..

We rejoice in the wondrous powers of our human minds and hearts, that we can remember and forecast and select our ways, that we can feel the hurt of others, that we may be ashamed and afraid, that we can laugh and sing and play, that we can reason together and together fashion a life of common good.

We rejoice that we have a part in the great web of life that holds us all, all suns and elements and every living thing. We rejoice that in all the world there is no wholly severed thing or separate creature. Yet we acknowledge that we have sought for separate goods and special favors, and that our selfish greeds have broken the great chain of being that holds all souls in life,

We remember those whose lands and homes have been despoiled by the cruelties of war and the rapacities of peace; and the brave of every race who seek true freedoms for their nations. May our own land be purged of those disrespects that dim the light of our example. May we learn anew how to give and how to receive. As they who till the soil wait upon the early and latter rain, so do we wait with thankful hearts for the abounding goods we cannot ourselves effect but only receive. As they who sow seeds and guide the plow put forth their labors in confidence and hope, we offer ourselves to perform those works of good that cannot be done save by our own doing.

PRAYER OF CONFESSION

Before the wonders of life, we acknowledge our failures to see and to revere; before the sanctities of life, we are ashamed of our disrespects and indignities; before the gifts of life, we own that we have made choice of lesser goods, and here today seek the gifts of the spirit; before the heroisms of life, we would be enlarged to new devotion.

FOR HEALTH AND WHOLENESS

O God of wholeness and truth, who ever moves to fashion all things complete and whole, in Your presence we see the imperfections around us; by Your light we are ashamed of the darkness of our own hearts. We have fallen short of the fulness of life that might be in us. We have not enough served the unfinished works of light in the world of many nations. Help us here to see the brightness of Your glory, that all our days we may steadfastly seek the health and wholeness of our comrades near and far.

WE CONFESS

Unseen Source of peace and holiness, we come into Your secret place to be filled with Your pure and solemn light. As we come to You, we remember that we have not walked lovingly with each other and humbly with You; that we have feared what is not terrible and wished for what is not holy. In our weakness, be the quickening power of life. Arise within our hearts as healing, strength, and joy. Day by day may we grow in faith, in charity, in the faith by which we see You, and in the larger life of love to which You call us.

WE REMEMBER

We turn to You, O Light and Life of humankind, for in Your light alone may we see the right and find the good. Here we remember those whose lives are darkened by the greed and wrong of others. We have not purged the commerce of our times of those harsh ways that hinder the hopes and dreams of many. We remember wars and rumors of war. We have made but feeble efforts to understand the peoples of the world and to foster peace among the nations. In this house of joy, we remember all sorrowing and troubled folk. Let us here be gathered into a common power of good will which shall issue in lasting peace.

OUT OF DARKNESS

We rejoice this day in the unquenchable and eternal light that lights everyone who comes into the world. In that light, we are ashamed of those greeds within us that have darkened our own souls, and those selfish customs among us that have shadowed the lives and spirits of others. We seek Your presence here, O Most High, not alone for our joy today, but to illumine the ways of all our doings until every child everywhere shall be brought out of darkness into Your marvelous light.

JOACHIM WACH

O HOLY ONE

Enlighten our minds, O Holy One, so we may understand each other and be saved from sterility of mind.

Fill us with a sense of the urgency of our task.

Save us from disabling despair and from undue optimism.

Help us to continue daily self-examination which prevents us from sinking into mere routine and enables us to understand the ever new quest for truth.

We seek encouragement not to falter in the light of disappointments and difficulties accompanying the confusions this day and age.

Guard us against subtle temptations to conform, to keep silent when we should stand up and speak.

May we hear the voice of our neighbor in all the narrower and wider communities of which we find ourselves members: the family, the local community, the nation, the continent, the region, the world.

Illuminate our minds so we may search for meaning in history and understand what You teach us.

May we find ways and means by which to communiicate a sense of Your presence in history to those who are entrusted to our care.

May we render service to the growing, worldwide movement of creative community.

WALT WHITMAN

SONG OF THE UNIVERSAL

Give me, O God, to sing;
Give me, give him or her I love this quenchless faith,
In your ensemble;
Whatever else witheld, withold not from us
Belief in plan of You enclosed in Time and Space,
Health, peace, salvation universal.

Is it a dream?
Nay but the lack of a dream,
And failing it life's lore and wealth a dream,
And all the world a dream.

GIVE ME THE SPLENDID SILENT SUN

Give me the splendid silent sun with all his beams full-dazzling,
Give me juicy autumnal fruit ripe and red from the orchard,
Give me a field where the unmowed grass grows,
Give me an arbor, give me the trellised grape,
Give me fresh corn and wheat, give me serene-moving animals teaching content,
Give me nights perfectly quiet as on high plateaus west of the Mississippi, and I looking up at the stars,
Give me odorous at sunrise a garden of beautiful flowers where I can walk undisturbed,
Give me for marriage a sweet-breathed woman of whom I should never tire,
Give me a perfect child, give me a way aside from the noise of the world, a rural domestic life,

Give me to warble spontaneous songs reclusive by myself,
Give me solitude, give me Nature, give me again, O Nature, your primal sanities!

HOW ADMIRABLE THE EARTH

How admirable—the cool-breathed earth!
Earth of the slumbering liquid trees!
Earth of departed sunsets!
Earth of the mountains!
Earth of the full moon tinged with blue!
Earth of the limpid grey of clouds!
Far-swooping, elbow'd earth!
Rich apple-blossomed earth!
How reverence-waking—the voluptuous earth!

How welcome all earth's lands, O God, each for its kind.
Welcome are lands of pine and oak.
Welcome are lands of the lemon and fig.
Welcome are lands of gold.
Welcome are lands of wheat and maize, welcome those of grape,
Welcome are lands of sugar and rice,
Welcome the cotton-lands, welcome those of the white potato and sweet potato,
Welcome are the mountains, flats, sands, forests, prairies,
Welcome the rich borders of rivers, table-lands, openings,
Welcome the measurelesss grazing-lands,
Welcome the teeming soil of orchards, flax, honey, hemp;
Welcome just as much are the other more hard-faced lands,
Lands rich as lands of gold or wheat and fruit lands,
Lands of mines, lands of manly and rugged ores,
Lands of coal, copper, lead, tin, zinc,
Lands of iron—lands of the make of the axe

How glad and firm the clasp of all earth's lands, to those who run to greet You in their presence.

I THANK YOU

I cannot rest, O God; I cannot eat or drink or slelep
Till I put forth myself, my prayer, once more to You,
Breathe, bathe myself once more in You, commune with You,
Report myself once more to You.

You know my years entire, my life,
My long and crowded life of active work, not adoration merely,
You know the prayers and vigils of my youth,
You know my later solemn and visionary meditations;
You know how, before I commenced, I devoted all to come to
You,
Accepting all from You, as duly comes from You.

All my undertakings have been filled with You:
The urge, the ardor, the unconquerable will.
O, I am sure they really came from You.
The end I know not; it is all in You.
You have lighted my life, O God,
With array of light, steady, ineffable,
Light rare untellable, lighting the very light,
Beyond all signs, descriptions, languages;
For that, O God, I thank You.

GOD

Why should I wish to see You better than this day?
I see something of You in each hour of the twenty-four, and each mo-
ment then;
In the faces of men and women I see You, and in my own face in the
glass.
I find letters from You dropped in the street, and every one is signed
by Your name;
And I leave them where they are, for I know that wheresoe'er I go,
Others will punctually come for ever and ever.

DAVID RHYS WILLIAMS

FOR FAMILIES

O God, whose home is the universe and whose universe is also our home: we lift up grateful hearts that the human race dwells together in families and that members of our families dwell together in trust and love. Bless us all—old and young, parents and children alike—in common cause.

WISDOM OF THE AGES

O Life, the great teacher of humanity: we are thankful that through sorrow we are taught the meaning of human sympathy; through suffering, we are led to learn the secret of patience; through defeat, the virtue of humility; through doubt, the creative power of faith; through loneliness, the worth of friendship; through toil, the value of leisure; and through sickness, the blessing of health.

Open our eyes to wisdom of the ages, lest we die before we have learned how to live.

ROGER WILLIAMS

YOU MAKE A PATH

You make a path, provide a guide
        And feed a wilderness;
Your glorious name, while breath remains,
        O that I may confess.

Lost many a time, I had no guide,
        No house but a hollow tree.
In stormy winter night no fire,
        No food, no company.

In You I found a house, a bed,
        A table, company;
No cup so bitter but's made sweet,
        Where You shall sweetening be.

LITANIES

THE VENERABLE THICH NHAT HAHN

A LITANY FOR PEACE

As we are together praying for Peace, let us be truly with each other.
Silence
Let us pay attention to our breathing.
Silence
Let us be relaxed in our bodies and our minds.
Silence
Let us return to ourselves and become wholly ourselves.
Silence
Let us be aware of the Source of Being common to us all and to all that is.
Silence
Evoking the presence of the Great Companion, let us fill our hearts with our own compassion—towards ourselves and toward all living beings.
Silence
Let us pray that all living beings realize that they are all nourished from the same Source of Life.
Silence
Let us pray that we ourselves cease to be the cause of needless suffering.
Silence
Let us pray that we may live in a way which will not needlessly deprive other living beings of air, water, food, shelter, or the chance to live in health.
Silence
With reverence for Life and with awareness of the sufferings that are going on around us, let us pray for the establishment of peace in our hearts and on earth.

ORDERS OF WORSHIP
FOR MANCHESTER COLLEGE, OXFORD

LITANY OF REMEMBRANCE

Almighty and eternal God, before whom stand the spirits of the living and the dead, we praise You for the wise of every land and age, and for all teachers of humanity:
We praise You, O God.

For the martyrs and faithful witnesses of whom the world was not worthy; and for all who have resisted falsehood and wrong unto suffering and death:
We praise You, O God.

For all who have labored and suffered for free choice, for good government and just laws; for all who have sought to lighten the burden of oppressed peoples in many places of the earth:
We praise You, O God.

For the dear friends and kindred of our homes whose faces we see no more, but whose love is with us forever; for the teachers and companions of our own childhood and youth, and the members of our household of faith who worked and worshiped with us:
We give thanks to You, O God.

We pray that we may hold them in continual remembrance; that their wisdom may rest upon us; and that we keep in fellowship both with the faithful and true of all ages and climes and with our beloved dead who dwell in peace:
We who now live and labor on earth unite in ascribing unto You, O God, all honor, dominion and power, worlds without end.

LITANY OF THANKSGIVING

Almighty God, from whom comes every good and perfect gift, we lift up our voices in thanksgiving. For all the gifts You have bestowed upon us, for the life You have given us, and for the world in which we live:
We praise You, O God.

For the work we are empowered to do; for the beauty and bounty of the world; for seed-time and harvest and the varied gifts each season brings:
We praise You, O God.

For all the gladness of life; for the comfort of home and the charm of companions:
We praise You, O God.

84

For the achievement of freedom in well ordered communities; for laws which advance justice and equality of opportunity; for education which enhances life through the arts and sciences of power:
We praise You, O God.

Through knowledge of You as we experience the world; for prophets and seers who are open to new truth; and for all lovers and helpers of humanity:
We praise You, O God.

For the disciplines of freedom which enlarge our souls; for endless opportunities to help those in need; for occasions of rest and relaxation which encourage us toward new adventure:
We praise You, O God, and will constantly praise You through all the days of our years.

ONE LIFE

Dear Deathless Power, the confidence of all the ends of the earth, and of them that are afar upon the sea and those who move in space: we would enlarge our faith that we may think of needs beyond our own.

We pray for all nations and their leaders that they may walk in the ways of justice and peace; for people of all faiths throughout the world, that they may be illumined by Your light and be guided by Your spirit;.

We pray our cities and towns, that those who govern may be wise and courageous, and that our citizens may so cultivate tolerance and reason that our differences may not deeply divide us, nor our practices dishonor us, nor our conflicts leave us embittered.

We pray for all who seek, day after day, to guide the opinions of people: for thinkers, writers, broadcasters, teachers, prophets, that inspired by realistically high ideals, they may communicate what is true and uphold what is just.

We pray for all artists and craftspeople, poets and musicians, who enrich the world with beauty and skill; for those who seek out nature and declare the wonders of our environment; that through their gifts and discoveries our common life may be enlarged and adorned.

We pray for all who buy and sell and get gain, that they seek no advantage for themselves that would hinder the good of all; for all who work in field or factory, office, laboratory or home, by whose labors we are clothed and fed; for all who toil beneath the earth or fly the pathway of the air; for all who go down to the sea in ships; for all men and women in their various callings, that they may have joy and gladness in their work.

Enable us to build a community of creative life on earth. Open our eyes that we may see the beauty of Your world and contribute to Your good works evermore.

PILGRIM HYMNAL

A LITANY OF LEARNING

Teacher of us all, we are thankful:

For those who transmit ancient wisdom;

For all who seek new truth, believing more light is yet to break forth;

For scientists looking upon the body of nature and seeing order in its variety;

For builders, poets, painters and makers of music who open our eyes and unstop our ears to Your beauty surrounding us always;

For all who would lead our thoughts beyond what is actual to what is waiting to be realized, that we may move toward fullness of life;

For all who bring their knowledge and their love to the service of humanity, providing vision without which we perish;

For all who labor to promote the growth of wisdom and knowledge in centers of living and learning, work and worship; that together we may foster the well-being of our family and friends, community and nation, continent, and planet and extra-terrestrial space.

PLAINS INDIAN PRAYER

GREAT GOD, WE SUMMON YOU

Great Spirit, who dwells in every object, every person and every place: we summon You from the far places into our present awareness.

God of the North, Who gives wings to the waters of the air and rolls out the snow-storm covering the earth with silver carpet: temper us with toughness to withstand the biting blizzard.

God of the East and of the red sun's rising, brace us that we neither neglect our gifts nor lose in laziness the hopes each day affords.

God of the South Whose warm breath of compassion dissolves our fears and meets our hatreds: teach us that they who are truly strong are also kind.

God of the West and of the sunset, bless us with knowledge of the freedom which follows the well-disciplined life.

God of the earth beneath our feet, storer of unreckoned resources: we would give thanks unceasingly for Your great bounty.

Great God within, may we be aware of the goodness of the gift of life and be worthy of its priceless privilege.

SERVICES FOR CONGREGATIONAL WORSHIP

A LITANY OF THANKS

O God, our true life, in whom and by whom all things live, who by Your spirit commands us to seek You, and are ever ready to be found; to know You is Life, to serve You is freedom to praise You is the joy and happiness of the soul.

We praise You and give thanks for Your greatness

For seasons of bounty and of beauty, for nights of quiet sleep, for days of health, for the glory of the earth and its ministry to our need;

We bless You, O God,

For all the generations before us who, through effort and pain, have wrought so that we might be heirs of liberty and truth and peace;

We thank You, and pray that we may enter into this heritage.

For new hopes of fairer life and nobler freedoms that stir the hearts of many people today;

We praise You, O God.

For the discipline that enriches, for the burden that strengthens, for the failure that is true success, and for the sorrow that enlarges the soul;

We give You thanks, O God,

For the soul, and its powers, for strong desires to fashion ourselves after Your likeness, and all our world into new orders of beauty and right;

We rejoice and give You thanks, and to You be the honor and the glory, worlds without end.

LITANY OF LOVE

O God, the source of all being and all joy, let Your blessings be upon us, and fill us with Your love.

From all jealousy and envy, from all unkindness, from offence given or taken, from unrighteous anger and an impatient spirit, from a hard and unforgiving temper, and from evil-speaking,
O God, deliver us.

From all ambition and greed which bring want and distress to multitudes and debase the bodies and souls of many, shutting from them the fulness of life.
O God, deliver us.

From an unquiet and discontented spirit, from despondency and gloom, from doubts of Your boundless love, and from forgetfulness of the manifold goods of Life,
O God, deliver us.

Inspire in us that spirit which suffers long and is kind; which envies not; vaunted not itself, is not puffed up; which does not behave unseemly, and seeks not its own.
Grant us to be filled with the fulness of Your spirit.

Quicken in us that charity which is not easily provoked, which thinks no evil, which rejoices not in iniquity, but rejoices in the truth; which bears all things, believes all things, hopes all things, endures all things; the charity which never fails;
That so by Your grace we may establish good will upon the earth.

O God, the Father and Mother of us all, who has breathed Your own spirit into Your children and made us to be one with each other as members of Your household: enable us to make Your house a refuge for every wounded spirit, a home for every aspiring soul.
Amid diversities of knowledge and of faith, may we be one in spirit, in affection, and in devotion to You.

SERVICES OF RELIGION

FREE NATION AND FREE WORLD

God, who has made us one nation out of many peoples, amid our diversities of race and tradition, unite us in a common love of freedom and in a high ambition for our national life.

Continue in us the pioneering spirit which led our fathers across the estranging sea and up held them in the wilderness.

Deepen in the people of this land a devotion to the common commonweal, so that we may open new doors of hope to the neglected and oppressed; cleanse our hearts from the greed which preys upon others; and deliver our politics from corruption.

Help us to establish this land in righteousness.

Endue with the spirit of wisdom those entrusted with authority, that there may be peace within our borders, and that we may stand among the nations of the earth an example of justice and a power of good will.

Let Your peace, O God, rule in all our hearts.

To every council where nations bring their hopes and fears, grant wisdom and mutual understanding, that distrust and hatred may be diminished, and a common law of justice be established.

Let peace, O God, prevail throughout the earth.

SOCIETY FOR PROMOTING CHRISTIAN KNOWLEDGE

PRAY FOR PEACE

Let us pray for the peace of the world: for diplomats and rulers that they may have wisdom and courage to improve international relationships by finding effective ways to reconcile people of different races, colors, conditions, and creeds; ...

Silence

Let us pray for men, women, and children the world over that they may have justice and freedom, and live in security and peace...

Silence

Let us pray for all who suffer as a result of war: for the injured and the disabled,for the mentally distressed, for those whose faith in God and humanity has been weakened or destroyed...

Silence

Let us pray for the homeless and refugees, for those who are hungry, for all who have lost their livelihood and security...

Silence

Let us pray for those who mourn their dead, for those who have lost husband or wife, children or parents...

Silence

We pray for the peace of the world.

A LITANY OF HOPE

Fountain of Hope within each breath and body;
Divine Deliverer from deepest loneliness, despair;
Source of eternal strength and inspiration:
> *Be our God, our living God.*

As You are Truth beyond all rigid prejudice:
Grant us to share Your free mind's open search.

As You are good beyond all selfish striving:
Grant us to share Your joy in giving love.

As You are Beauty known beyond our turmoil:
Grant us a vision of Your radiance unexcelled.

As You are free, with urge toward healthy growing:
Grant us to rise toward the unattained.

> Where there is sorrow, may we bring comfort;
> *Where there is sickness, health;*
> Where there is false fear, trust;
> *Where there is conflict, courage;*
> Where there is envy, appreciation;
> *Where there is needless war, peace.*

Source of eternal strength and inspiration:
Be our rock, our dayspring, and our joy.

VON OGDEN VOGT

THE MANIFOLD RICHNESS OF LIFE

Let us rejoice in the manifold richness of life, about us and within: within us as an understanding and choice, about us as a fair and bountiful nature, and the works of generous souls;

We rejoice in the abundant life.

In the immemorial story of humankind; of struggle and venture, of sowing and reaping, of mirth and zest, of rites and assemblies, of mating and feasting, of ordered custom and new liberties won;

We rejoice in the story of humanity.

In the finding of facts and in shapes of molded form, in motions of the dance and of melody, in storied images of grief and ecstasy, in new visions of order.

We rejoice in the beauty of art and the power of knowledge.

For the rest of home, the comfort of friends, and the unending charm of persons; for the desire to work and to create, for the broad earth and the affairs of toil open before us.

We are thankful for home and friends and life's labor.

For prophets and reformers who cry shame upon social wrong, for leaders of the people who are wise in the policies of state, for many forms of effort to build a commonwealth where all souls may reach their highest good: we are thankful.

Let us cherish the state that mighty ends may be achieved.

For shrines of faith where goods are praised and evils faced, where sorrows are healed and high purposes kindled, where our spirits are brought to that accord with all things which is at once our noblest task and most sublime joy: we are thankful.

Let us upbuild the church in strength to minister ever more abundant life and peace to all the world.

LITANY OF LEARNING

Almighty and eternal God, Source of the light that never sets and of the love that never fails, Life of our life: draw us to Yourself in trust and love.

By all the wonder and the meaning of Your order which rules over all; by the beauty which shines through all; by the ever wider knowledge and deeper life which blesses all:

Teach us and lead us ever nearer to You.

By the revelation of Yourself in the lives of all wise, great and good women and men; by the strength and grace which shine for us in the founders of great ways of life; by every living word of truth and every good example:

Teach us and lead us ever nearer to You.

By the kindness and love which have been with us from the beginning of our days, even until now; by the relations of home and the love of little children; by the faithful loyalty of friends; by the very trials and bereavements which chasten and deepen our lives; by all the blessed memories of our dead:

Teach us and lead us every nearer to You,

By the deeds of brave and generous leaders, who labor for a more just industry and a nobler state for all our people; by the vision of those who seek a fairer world for the people of other lands and peace among all nations:

Teach us and lead us ever nearer to You.

By all our experience; in health and in sickness; in joy and in sorrow; in every circumstance and in every place, O God, our Father and Mother Eternal:

Teach us and lead us ever nearer to You.

LITANY OF REJOICING

Bright Joy, Bright Joy: the joy of flowers and shining sun, the joy of smiles and play and dancing.
We rejoice in the good of nature.
Lovely Things, Beautiful Shapes and sounds: the shapes of houses and carven stones, the shapes of words together, the sounds of songs and sounds of many woven voices, winding, rhythmic.
We rejoice in the human artifice.
Darkness and Night: the dark of pain, the fret of baffling malady, the last dark, the dark of death.
We know the perils and pains of nature's body.
Gloom and Deeper Gloom: the dim dark of knowledge never known, of spirits unillumined, the darker gloom of light denied, the dark of mercy quenched and comrades condemned.
We acknowledge the shame of evil within.
Mighty Humanity, Inventive Humanity: creator of tools and wheels, of dynamos and wings, of computation and exploration of space.
We rejoice in the masteries of humanity.
Noble Leaders, Stately Leaders: leaders of freedom and order, leaders painting new designs of thought, leaders uniting nations and citizens in durable peace amidst healthy strife.
We rejoice in the world order that is, and in nobler orders dreamed.
Folly, Wasteful Folly: the folly of war and greed, the ruin of bodies, the waste of brains, the folly of riches that stifle alike those who have not and those who have.
We acknowledge our share of guilt in the wastage of life.
Feeble Life, Futile Life: the life of pride, pride of place and pride of learning, life falsely free that draws away from common songs and common prayers.
We seek free associations that inspire people's hopes.
Humanity Generous, Humanity Uplifted: those who lay down their lives for their friends, who give themselves that a new spirit may arise in the world.
We also would walk in newness of life.
Sublime Truth, Healing Truth: light that is light, and darkness turned to light, joy that is joy, and sorrow turned to joy.
We seek this truth for ourselves, that pain and loss may yet be turned to grace and good.
Life Before, Life Beyond, Life Within: the human spirit overcoming obstacles, the revering of the fountain forces whence we came; we on earth hoping, daring—and range on range of life beyond our power.
We rejoice in wondrous good received and good performed, and we commit ourselves with trust and zeal to that unfolding Life that holds us all.

LITANY OF GRATEFULNESS

Let us join in grateful praise for the goods of life that our ours.

With the voices and hearts of all the children of humanity, with seers and prophets, with those whose craftmanship is their song, with all who find in human service their joy made full;

We lift up our hearts in gratitude and praise.

In life; its adventures, risks and prizes; in the strength of the soul that overcomes all dangers;

We rejoice with thanksgiving.

In tasks that are hard; in work well done; in the skill of our hands; in experience, judgment, decision;

We rejoice with thanksgiving.

In knowledge; in joining fact to fact; in seeing truth in its beauty;

We rejoice with thanksgiving.

In health; in sickness that has passed away; in sorrows that have not visited us; in temptation that did not tarry at our door; in fears that turned to triumph;

We rejoice with thanksgiving.

In the faces of those we love; in the eyes that look kindly upon us even when we fail; in those with whom we are at rest;

We rejoice with thanksgiving.

In those who, though dead, yet speak, the known and the unknown, the great and the lowly, by whose lives we are enabled to live;

We rejoice and will rejoice forevermore.

Let the work of our hands declare the gladness of our hearts, and kindly deeds speak forth the gratitude within.

LITANY OF ABUNDANT LIVING

Let us rejoice in the manifold richness of life about us and within; within us as understanding and choice; about us a fair and bountiful nature and the works of generous women and men:

We rejoice in the abundant life.

In the immemorial story of human kind; of struggle and venture, of sowing and reaping, of mirth and zest, of rites and assemblies, of mating and feasting, of ordered custom and new liberties won:

We rejoice in the story of humanity.

In the finding of facts and in shapes of moulded form, in motions of the dance and of melody, in storied images of grief and of ecstasy, in new visions of order:

We rejoice in the beauty of art and the power of knowledge.

For the rest of home, the comfort of friends and the unending charm of persons; for the desire to work and create; for the broad earth and the affairs of toil open before us.

We are thankful for home and friends and life's labor.

For prophets and reformers who cry shame upon social wrong; for leaders of the people who are wise in the policies of state; for many forms of effort to build a commonwealth where everyone may reach the highest good; we are thankful

Let us cherish the state that her mighty ends may be achieved.

For shrines of faith where goods are praised and evils faced, where sorrows are healed and high purposes kindled, where our spirits are brought to that accord with all things which is at once our noblest task and most sublime joy; we are thankful.

Let us upbuild our household of faith in strength to minister ever more abundant life and peace to all the world.

PSALMS

THIRST FOR GOD

As the deer pants after the waterbrook,
So pants my soul after You, O God;
My soul thirsts for You, the living God.
When shall I see Your face, O God.

My tears are my meat day and night,
While they say to me continually, "Where is You God?"
As with a sword in my bones, my enemies reproach me,
While they say daily to me, "Where now is Your God?"
When I remember these things, I pour out my soul.
Why am I cast down?
Why am I disquieted within?

I hope in You; I shall always praise You, O God, my
    health.
Deep calls to deep at the noise of Your waterspouts;
All Your waves and billows go over me.
You command loving kindness in the day time,
In the night, a song to You shall be with me,
And a prayer to You, the God of my life.

THE NATIONS PRAISE YOU

God, be gracious to us and bless us
        And make Your face to shine upon us:
        That Your way may be known upon the earth,
Your saving power among all nations.

Let the people praise You, O God,
Let all people praise You!
Let the nations be glad and sing for joy.
        For You judge the peoples with equity,
        And govern the nations upon the earth
Let all the people praise You, O God;
Let all the people praise You.
        The earth has yielded its increase:
        You, O our God, have blessed us.

A PSALM OF THANKSGIVING

God of our salvation, You are the confidence of all
    the ends of the earth,
And of them that are afar off in space or on the sea:
Your strength established the mountains;
You still the tumult of the people.
You visit the earth and water it;
You enrich it and provide grain.
You water its furrows abundantly,
Softening it with showers and blessing its growth.
You crown the year with Your bounty
The little hills rejoice on every side.
The meadows are clothed with flocks:
They shout and sing together for joy.

HAVE MERCY UPON ME

Have mercy upon me, O God, according to Your loving kindness;
According to the multitude of Your tender mercies, blot out my
transgressions.

I acknowledge my transgressions;
And my sin is before me.
    Against You, You only have I sinned,
    And done what is evil in Your sight.
Hide Your face from my sins,
And blot out all my iniquities.
    Create in me a clean heart, O God;
    And renew a right spirit within me.
Cast me not away from Your presence;
And take not Your holy spirit from me.
    Restore unto me the joy of Your salvation;
    And uphold me with Your free spirit.
Deliver me from my transgressions, O God;
And my tongue shall sing aloud of Your righteousness.
    Open my lips, O God,
    And my mouth shall show forth Your praise.
You desire not sacrifice, else would I give it;
You delight not in burnt offering.
    The sacrifices You desire are a broken spirit;
    A broken and a contrite heart, O God, You will not despise.

HEAR MY CRY

Hear my cry, O God.
Listen to my prayer.
From the ends of the earth, I call to You when my heart is faint.
Lead me to the rock that is higher than I.
You have been my refuge, a strong tower against the foe.
I will ever sing praises to Your name.

HEAR MY PRAYER

Hear my prayer, O God;
Let my cry come to You!
Do not hide Your face from me in my day of distress!
Incline Your ear to me; answer speedily when I call!
My days pass away like smoke, and my bones burn like a furnace.
My heart is smitten like grass and withered;
I forget to eat my bread;
My bones cleave to my flesh.
I am like a vulture of the wilderness, like an owl of the waste
    places;
I lie awake, I am like a lonely bird on the housetop.
I eat ashes like bread, and mingle tears with my drink,
For You have taken me up and thrown me away.
My days are like an evening shadow;
I wither away like grass.
But You, O God, are enthroned for ever;
Your name endures to all generations.
Of old You laid the foundation of the earth
And the heavens are the work of Your hands.
They will perish but You endure;
They will all wear out like a garment
You change them like a raiment, and they pass away;
But You are the same, and Your years have no end.
The children of Your servants shall dwell secure;
Their posterity shall be established before You.

DAY UNTO DAY

The heavens declare Your glory, O God.
And the firmament proclaims Your handiwork.
Day unto day pours forth speech,
And night unto night shows knowledge
There is not speech or language
Where their voice is not heard.
Their line is gone out through all the earth,
And their words to the end of the world.
In them You set a tent for the sun,
Which like a strong racer runs its course with joy.
Its rising is from the end of the heavens,
And there is nothing hid from its heat.
Your law is perfect, reviving the soul;
Your testimony is is sure, making wise the simple,
Your statutes are right, rejoicing the heart;
Your commandment is pure, enlightening the eyes.
Our fear of You is clean, enduring forever;
Your judgements are true and righteous altogether.
More to be desired are they than gold, even much fine gold.
Sweeter also than honey and the honeycomb.
Moreover, by them, is Your servant warned;
And in keeping of them there is great reward.
Who can understand his of her errors?
Cleanse me from secret faults.
Keep me also from presumptuous sins;
Let them not have dominion over me.
May the words of my mouth, and the meditations of my heart,
Be acceptable in Your sight, O God, my strength and my redeemer.

I EXTOL YOU

I extol You, O God, for You lifted me up from the pit.
I cried unto You, and You healed me.
I sing unto You and give thanks for Your help.
I cry unto You, and You turn my mourning into dancing.
I will give thanks to You forever.

YOU ARE MY GOD

In You, O God, do I put my trust.
You are my rock and my fortress:
Therefore, lead me, and guide me.
Into Your hand I commit my spirit;
For You have considered my trouble:
You have known my soul in adversities.
I trust in You, O God:
You are my God.
O how great is Your goodness,
Which You have wrought for those who trust
in You.
We love You, O God;
All of my hope is in You.

SING FOR JOY

It is good to give thanks and to sing praises
to You, O Most High;
To declare Your steadfast love in the morning
and Your faithfulness every night.
You have made me glad by Your work;
At the works of Your hands, I sing for joy.

EVERY DAY

I will extol You every day, O God;
I will praise You forever and ever.
Great are You and greatly to be praised;
Indeed, Your greatness is unsearchable.
One generation shall praise Your works to another,
And shall declare Your mighty acts.
You are gracious and merciful;
Slow to anger, full of lovingkindness.
You are good to all,
And Your tender mercies are over all Your works.
Your kingdom is an everlasting kingdom,
And Your dominion endures through all generations.

THE MEASURE OF MY DAYS

God, make me to know my end, and what is the measure of
    my days
That I may know how frail I am.
    Behold Your have made my days a few handbreadths.
    And my lifeline is as nothing in Your sight.
Surely everyone stands as a mere breath!
Surely everyone goes about as a shadow!
    Surely everyone walks in a vain show!
    We heap up riches and know not who will gather them.
And now, O God, for what do I wait?
My hope is in You.
    Hear my prayer, and give ear to my cry;
    Hold not Your peace at my tears.
Put a new song in my mouth,
A song of praise unto You, O God.
    I am Your passing guest, a sojourner like my mother
      and father.
    May I know gladness before I depart and am no more.

YOUR WONDERFUL WORKS

Many are the wonderful works You have done;
None can compare with You!
  Were I to proclaim and tell of them,
  They would be more than can be numbered.
I have told the glad news of deliverance to the great congregation;
I have not restrained my lips, as You know.
  I have spoken of Your faithfulness and Your salvation;
  I have not concealed Your steadfast love and Your faithfulness.
May all who seek You rejoice and be glad in You;
May those who love You say continually, "Great is God!"
  Do not withhold Your tender mercies from me, O God;
  May Your loving kindness and Your truth preserve me.

DEFEND MY CAUSE

O God, defend my cause.
Deliver me from unjust and deceitful people.
You are the God in whom I take refuge.
Why have You cast me off?
Why am I in mourning because of the oppression of the
 enemy?
Send out Your light and Your truth.
Let them lead me.
Let them bring me to Your sanctuary.
Then will I go to Your altar, O God,
I will praise You with exceeding joy, O God, my help.

HOW EXCELLENT IS YOUR NAME

O God, our God,
How excellent is Your name in all the earth.
 When I consider the heavens, the work of Your fingers,
 The moon and the stars which You ordained:
Who are we, that You are mindful of us,
Or our children's children that Your should care for them?
 O God, our God,
 How excellent is Your name in all the earth.

YOU ARE MY GOD

O God, You are my God:
Early will I seek You:
 My soul thirsts for You,
 As in a dry and weary land where no water is.
I have looked upon You in the sanctuary,
Beholding Your power and Your glory.
 Because Your steadfast love is better than life,
 My mouth will praise You with joyful lips.
I will bless You as long as I live:
I will lift up my hands and call on Your name.
 Because You have been my help,
 I will sing for joy in the shadow of Your wings.

THE UNESCAPABLE GOD

O God, You have searched me and known me!
You know my downsitting and my uprising;
    You discern my thoughts from afar;
    You search out my path and my lying down,
And are acquainted with all my ways.
You have beset me behind and before,
And laid Your hand upon me.
    Such knowledge is too wonderful for me;
    It is high, I cannot attain it.
Whither shall I go from Your spirit,
Or whither shall I flee from Your presence?
    If I ascend to heaven, You are there;
    If I make my bed in the grave, behold, You are there.
And dwell in the uttermost parts of the sea,
    Even there Your hand shall lead me,
    And Your right hand shall hold me.
If I say, "Surely the darkness shall cover me,"
Even the night shall be light about me;
    Yea, the darkness does not hide from You,
        but the night shines as the day:
    The darkness and the light are both alike to You.

    You formed my inward parts;
You knit me together in my mother's womb.
    I will praise You, for I am fearfully and wonderfully made.
    Marvelous are Your works, and that my soul well knows.

How precious to me are Your thoughts, O God!
How vast the sum of them!
    If I should count them, they are more in number than the
        sand;
    When I awake I am still with You.
Search me, O God, and know my heart!
Try me and know my thoughts!
    And see if there be any wicked way in me,
    And lead me in the way everlasting!

OUT OF THE DEPTHS

Out of the depths have I cried unto You.
O God, hear my voice:
Be attentive to my prayers.
If You should mark iniquities,
O God, who could stand?
But there is forgiveness with You,
That You may be revered.
I wait for You; my soul waits,
And in Your word I hope.
My soul waits for You, O God,
More than they who watch for the morning:
I say, more than they who watch for the morning.
For with You there is steadfast love,
And with You is plenteous redemption.

HELP IN TROUBLE

You are our refuge and our strength, O God,
A very present help in trouble.

Therefore, we will not fear, though the earth be removed,
And though the mountains be shaken into the seas;
Though the waters thereof roar and be troubled;
Though the mountains tremble with the swelling thereof.

I TRUST IN YOU

Unto You, O God, I lift up my soul.
O my God, I trust in You;
Let me not be ashamed
Let none that wait for You be ashamed;
Let them be ashamed who are wantonly treacherous.
Show me You ways, O God:
Teach me Your paths.
Lead me in Your truth, and teach me;
For You are the God of my salvation:
For You I wait all the day long.
Remember, O God, Your tender mercies
And Your loving kindness;
For they have been ever of old.
All Your paths are mercy and truth
Unto such as keep Your covenant.

YOU ARE MY LIGHT

You are my light, O God;
    Whom shall I fear?
You are the strength of my life;
    Of whom shall I be afraid?

Though enemies should encamp against me,
    My heart shall not fear.
Though war should rise against me,
    Through You will I be confident.

I have sought one thing from You,
    And that will I seek:
That I may dwell in Your house,
    Beholding the beauty of our world.

In the time of trouble,
    You will be my Rock.
When I cry out in pain,
    You will suffer with me in my woe.

You are my help, O God;
    You will not forsake me.
If my father and my mother forsake me,
    You will take me up.

Teach me You way,
    And lead me in a plain path.
I would have fainted had I not believed I would see Your
    goodness in the land of the living.

THE ENDS OF THE EARTH

You bless us, O God,
And cause Your face to shine upon us.
May Your way be known upon the earth,
Your saving power among all nations.
May the whole world praise You;
May all races praise You;
May all nations be glad and sing for joy,
For You rule the world justly;
You guide the nations of the earth!
The people praise You, O God;
All the people praise You!
The earth has yielded its increase;
You, O God, bless us.
May everyone revere You to the ends of the earth!

THE DAYS OF OUR YEARS

You have been our dwelling-place in all generations,
    O God.
Before the mountains came forth,
And before the earth was formed,
Even from everlasting to everlasting, You are God.
You turn us to destruction saying,
Return, You children of the earth.
A thousand years in Your sight
Are but as yesterday when it is past,
And as a watch in the night.
You carry them away as with a flood;
They are as asleep.
In the morning, they are like grass which flourishes and
    grows;
In the evening, it is cut down and withers.
The days of our years are three-score years and ten;
But even if they be fourscore years of more,
Their pride becomes labor and sorrow,
For it is soon gone, and we fly away.
So teach us to number our days,
That we may apply our hearts to wisdom.

HYMNS

MONROE BEARDSLEY

THE VOICE WITHIN

From all the fret and fever of the day,
Let there be moments when we turn away,
And, deaf to all confusing outer din,
Intently listen for the voice within.

In quietness and solitude, we find
The soundless wisdom of the deeper mind;
With clear harmonious purpose let us then
Bring richer meaning to the world again.

WILLIAM BLAKE

TO MERCY, PITY, PEACE AND LOVE

To Mercy, Pity, Peace and Love
All pray in their distress
And to those virtues of delight
Return their thankfulness.

For Mercy, Pity, Peace and Love
Is You, our God most dear;
And Mercy, Pity, Peace and Love
Is Man, Your child and care.

For Mercy has a human heart,
Pity, a human face;
And Love, the human form divine,
And Peace, the human dress.

Then ev'ry one, of ev'ry clime,
That prays in true distress,
Prays to the human form divine:
Love, Mercy, Pity, Peace.

And all must love the human form
In heathen, Turk or Jew;
Where Mercy, Love, and Pity dwell,
There You are dwelling too.

ELEANOR FARJRON

MORNING HAS BROKEN

Morning has broken
Like the first morning,
Blackbird has spoken
Like the first bird.
Praise for the singing!
Praise for the morning!
Praise for them, springing
Fresh from the Word!

Sweet the rain's new fall
Sunlit from heaven,
Like the first dewfall
On the first grass.
Praise for the sweetness
Of the wet garden,
Sprung in completeness
Where Your feet pass.

Mine is the sunlight!
Mine is the morning
Born of the one light
Eden saw play!
Praise with elation,
Praise every morning,
Your re-creation
Of the new day!

HARRY EMERSON FOSDICK

GOD OF GRACE AND GOD OF GLORY

God of grace and God of glory,
On Your people pour Your power;
Crown Your ancient church's story;
Bring its bud to glorious flower.
Grant us wisdom, grant us courage
For the facing of this hour.

Lo, the clouds of evil 'round us
Hide Your brightness from our gaze;
From the fears that long have bound us,

Free our hearts to trust and praise.
Grant us wisdom, grant us courage,
For the living of these days.

Cure Your children's warring madness;
Bend our pride to Your control;
Shame our wanton, selfish gladness,
Rich in things and poor in soul.
Grant us wisdom, grant us courage,
In our seeking to be whole.

Fill us with a living vision;
Heal our wounds that we may be
Bound as one beyond division
In the struggle to be free.
Grant us wisdom, grant us courage;
Ears to hear and eyes to see.

PAUL GERHARDT

EVENING

The duteous day now closes;
    Each flower and tree reposes;
Shade creeps o'er wild and wood.
    Let us, as night is falling,
On You, our Maker calling,
    Give thanks to You, the Giver good.

Now all the heav'nly splendor
    Breaks forth in starlight tender
From myriad worlds unknown;
    And we, Your marvel seeing,
Forget our selfish being
    For joy of beauty not our own.

EDWARD GRUBB

GIVE US OPEN EYES

Our God, to whom we turn
When weary with illusion,
Whose stars serenely burn
Above this earth's confusion:
Yours is the mighty plan,
The steadfast order sure,
In which the world began,
Endures, and shall endure.

You are Yourself the Truth;
Though we who fain would find You
Have tried, with thoughts uncouth,
In feeble words to bind You.
It is because You're best
We're driven to our quest;
Till truth from falsehood part
Our souls can find no rest.

Your Beauty speaks to me:
The mountains and the rivers,
The line of lifted sea,
Where spreading moonlight quivers.

The deep-toned organ blast
That rolls through arches dim
Hints of the music vast
Of Your eternal hymn.

Wherever good lurks
We catch Your tones appealing.
Where earth for justice works
You are Yourself revealing.
The blood of woman, man
On friendship's altar spilt
Betrays the mystic plan
On which Your house is built.

O hidden Fount of Love,
Of Peace and Truth and Beauty,
Inspire us from above
With joy and strength for duty.

May Your fresh light arise
Within each clouded heart,
And give us open eyes
To see You and Your art.

JOHN HAYNES HOLMES

THE VOICE OF GOD

Your voice, O God, is calling
    Its summons unto all;
As once You spoke in Zion,
    So now we hear You call:
Whom shall I send to succor
    My people in their need?
Whom shall I send to loosen
    The bonds of shame and greed?

I hear my people crying
    In cot and mine and slum;
No field or mart is silent,
    No city street is dumb.
I see my people falling
    In darkness and despair.
Whom shall I send to shatter
    The fetters which they bear?

We heed, O God, Your summons,
    And answer: Here are we!
Send us upon Your errand!
    Let us Your servants be!
Our strength is dust and ashes,
    Our years a passing hour;
But You can use our weakness
    To magnify our power.

From ease and plenty save us,
    From pride of place absolve;
Purge us of low desire,
    Lift us to high resolve.
Take us and make us holy,
    Teach us Your will and way;
Speak, and behold we answer!
    Command, and we obey!

JOHN HOLMES

O GOD OF STARS AND SUNLIGHT

O God of stars and sunlight,
  Whose wind lifts up a bird,
In marching wave and leaf fall,
  We hear Your patient word.
The color of the seasons
  Goes gold across the land.
By green upon the tree tops,
  We know Your moving hand.

O God of cloud and mountain,
  Whose rain on rock is art,
Your plan and care and meaning
  Renew the head and heart.
Your word and color spoken,
  Your summer noons and showers —
By these and by Your sunshine,
  We know Your world is ours.

O God of root and shading
  Of boughs above our head,
We breathe in Your long breathing
  Our spirit spirited.
We walk beneath Your blessing
  Your seasons and Your way,
O God of stars and sunlight,
  O God of this year's day.

WILLIAM DE WITT HYDE

IN THE MAKING

Creation's God, we give You thanks
  That this Your world is incomplete;
That battle calls our marshalled ranks,
  That work awaits our hands and feet;

That we are not yet fully wise,
  That we are in the making still, —
As friends who share one enterprise
  And strive to blend with nature's will.
Beyond the present sin and shame,

Wrong's bitter, cruel, scorching blight,
We seek the beckoning vision flame,
The blessed kingdom of the right.

What though the kingdom long delay,
And still with haughty foes must cope?
It gives us that for which to pray,
A field for toil and faith and hope.
Since what we choose is what we are,
And what we love we yet shall be,
The goal may ever shine afar, —
The will to win it makes us free.

JAMES WELDON JOHNSON

GOD OF OUR WEARY YEARS

God of our weary years,
God of our silent tears,
You who have brought us thus far on the way;
You who have by Your might
Led us into the light,
Keep us forever in the path, we pray.

Lest our feet stray from the places, our God,
Where we meet You;
Lest our hearts, drunk with the wine of the world,
We forget You;
Shadowed beneath Your hand,
May we forever stand
True to our God,
True to our native land.

DANIEL BEN JUDAH

YIGDAL

Praise to You, Living God,
All praised be Your name,
Who was, and is, and is to be,
For aye the same.
The one eternal God,
Ere ought that now appears:
The First, the Last, beyond all thought
Your timeless years.

Formless, all lovely forms
Declare Your loveliness;
Holy, all holiness of earth
Does Yours express.
Lo, You are God of all!
Creation speaks Your praise
And everywhere above, below,
Your will obeys.

Your spirit now flows free,
High surging where it will:
In prophet's word You spoke of old, —
And You speak still.
Established is Your law,
And changeless it shall stand,
Deep writ upon the human heart
On sea or land.

Eternal life You have
Implanted in the soul;
Your love shall be our strength and stay
While ages roll.
Praise be to You, O God!
All praised be Your name,
Who was, and is, and is to be
For aye the same!

SAMUEL LONGFELLOW

GOD OF THE EARTH

God of the earth, the sky, the sea;
    Maker of all above, below:
Creation lives in You and me;
    Your present life through all does flow.

Your love is in the sunshine's glow;
    Your life is in the quickening air;
When lightnings flash and storm-winds blow,
    There is Your power, Your law is there.

We feel Your calm at evening's hour,
    Your grandeur in the march of night;
And when the morning breaks in power,
    We hear Your word, "Let there be light!"

But higher far, and far more clear,
    You in our spirit we behold;
Your image and Yourself are there —
    Indwelling God, proclaimed of old.

LIGHT OF AGES AND OF NATIONS

Light of ages and of nations,
    Every race and every time
Has received Your inspirations,
    Glimpses of Your truth sublime.
Always spirits in rapt vision
    Passed the heavenly veil within,
Always hearts bowed in contrition
    Found salvation from their sin.

Reason's noble aspiration
    Truth in growing clearness saw;
Conscience spoke its condemnation,
    Or proclaimed the eternal law.
While Your inward revelations
    Told Your saints their prayers were heard,
Prophets to the guilty nations
    Spoke Your everlasting word.

Lo, that word abides forever;
    Revelation is not sealed;
Answering now to our endeavor,
    Truth and right are still revealed.
That which came to ancient sages,
    Greek, Barbarian, Roman, Jew,
Written in the soul's deep pages,
    Shines today forever new.

'TIS WINTER NOW

"Tis winter now: the fallen snow
    Has left the heav'ns all coldly clear;
Thro' leafless boughs the sharp winds blow,
    And all the earth lies dead and drear.

O God, Your love is not withdrawn:
    Your life within the keen air breathes;
Your beauty paints the crimson dawn,
    And clothes the boughs with glitt'ring wreaths.

And though abroad the sharp winds blow,
    And skies are chill, and frosts are keen,
Home closer draws her circle now,
    And warmer glows her light within.

O God, who gives the winter's cold,
    As well as summer's joyous rays,
Us warmly in Your love enfold
    And keep us through life's wintry days.

JOACHIM NEANDER

ALL MY HOPE

All my hope on You is founded;
    You, dear God, my trust renew;
Me through change and chance You pilot,
    Only good and only true.
        Deeply known,
        You alone
Call my heart to be Your own.

Pride of man and earthly glory,
    Sword and crown betray Your trust:
What with care and toil we build here,
    Tower and temple fall to dust.
        But Your power
        Hour by hour
Is my temple and my tower.

Your great goodness endures always,
    Deep Your wisdom passing thought:
Splendor, light and life attend You,
    Beauty springs up out of naught.
        Evermore
        From Your store
New born worlds rise and adore.

PRAISE BE TO YOU

Praise be to You, the Almighty, the God of creation;
My soul will praise You, for You are my health and salvation:
    All you who hear,
    Brothers and sisters,draw near,
Join in the glad adoration.

Praise be to You, who does prosper our work and defend us;
Surely Your goodness and mercy here daily attend us:
    We see anew
    What You, Almighty, can do,
Who with Your love does befriend us.

Praise be to You, O let all that is in us adore You!
All that has life and breath come now with praises before You!
    Let the Amen
    Sound from Your people again:
Gladly for eye we adore You.

PHILIPP NICOLAI

NOW LET EVERY TONGUE ADORE YOU

Now let every tongue adore You!
Let all together sing before You!
Let harps and cymbals now unite!
All Your deeds of love are glorious,
Where we partake through faith victorious,
With loved ones round Your throne of light.
　　No mortal eye has seen,
　　No mortal ear has heard
　　More wondrous things.
　　Therefore, with joy
　　Our song shall soar
In praise to You forevermore.

JOHN OXENHAM

NO EAST OR WEST

In God there is no East or West,
　　In You no South or North;
But one great fellowship of love
　　Throughout the whole wide earth.

In You do true hearts everywhere
　　Their high communion find;
Your service is the golden chord
　　Close-binding humankind.

Join hands, then, comrades of the faith,
　　Whate'er your race may be:
Who serves our Maker faithfully
　　Is surely kin to me.

In You now meet both East and West,
　　In You meet South and North;
All human souls are one in You
　　Throughout the whole wide earth.

FOLLIOTT SANDFORD PIERPOINT

FOR THE BEAUTY OF THE EARTH

For the beauty of the earth,
For the splendor of the skies,
For the love which from our birth
Over and around us lies:
Source of all, to You we raise
This our hymn of grateful praise.

For the joy of ear and eye,
For the heart and mind's delight,
For the mystic harmony
Linking sense to sound and sight:
Source of all, to You we raise
This our hymn of grateful praise.

For the wonder of each hour
Of the day and of the night,
Hill and vale and tree and flower,
Sun and moon an stars of light:
Source of all, to You we raise
This our hymn of grateful praise.

MARTIN RINKART

NOW THANK WE ALL OUR GOD

Now thank we all our God
    With hearts and hands and voices.
Who wondrous things has done,
    In whom the world rejoices.
You, from our mothers' arms
    Have blessed us on our way
With countless gifts of love.
    And still are ours today.

O may You, bounteous God,
    Through all our life be near us,
With ever joyful hearts
    And blessed peace to cheer us;
The one eternal God
    Whom heaven and earth adore,
For thus it was, is now,
    And shall be evermore.

DOROTHY L. SAYERS

HYMN IN CONTEMPLATION OF SUDDEN DEATH

God, if this day my journey end,
I thank You first for many a friend,
The sturdy and unquestioned piers
That run beneath my bridge of years.

Next, for the power You've given me
To view the whole world mirthfully,
For laughter, paraclete of pain,
Like April suns across the rain.

Also that, being not too wise
To do things foolish in folks' eyes,
I gained experience by this,
And saw life somewhat as it is.

Next for the joy of labor done
And burdens shouldered in the sun;
Not less, for shame of labor lost,
And meekness born of a barren boast.

For every fair and useless thing
That bids us pause from laboring
To look and find the larkspur blue
And marigolds of a different hue;

For eyes to see and ears to hear,
For tongue to speak and thews to bear,
For hands to handle, feet to go,
For life, I give You thanks also.

For all things merry, quaint and strange,
For sound and silence, strength, and change,
At last, for death, which only gives
Value to everything that lives;

For these, good God, who still makes me,
I praise Your name; since, verily,
I of my joy have had no dearth,
Though this day were my last on earth.

VINCENT B. SILLIMAN

MORNING SO FAIR TO SEE

Morning, so fair to see,
　　　Night veiled in mystery—
Glorious the earth and resplendent skies!
　　　Great God, we march along,
Singing our pilgrim song,
　　　As through an earthly paradise.

Fair are the verdant trees,
　　　Fair are the flashing seas,
Fair is each wonder the seasons bring.
　　　Fairer is faith's surmise
Shining in pilgrim eyes:
　　　Fairer the comradeship we sing.

Age after age we rise,
　　　'Neath the eternal skies,
Into the light from the shadowed past:
　　　Still shall our pilgrim song,
Buoyant and brave and strong
　　　Resound while we and mountains last.

JAN STRUTHER

WE THANK YOU

We thank You, God of heaven,
　　　For all the joys that greet us,
For all that You have given
　　　To help us and delight us
In earth and sky and seas;
　　　The sunlight on the meadows,
The rainbow's fleeting wonder,
　　　The clouds with cooling shadows,
The stars that shine in splendor—
　　　We thank You, God, for these.

For swift and gallant horses,
      For lambs in pastures springing,
For dogs with friendly faces,
      For birds with music thronging
Their chantries in the trees;
      For herbs to cool our fever,
For flowers of field and garden,
      For bees among the clover
With stolen sweetness laden—
      We thank You, God, for these.

For homely dwelling places
      Where childhood's visions linger,
For friends and kindly voices,
      For bread to stay our hunger
And sleep to bring us ease;
      For zeal and zest of living,
For faith and understanding,
      For words to tell our loving,
For hope of peace unending —
      We thank You, God, for these.

LOUIS UNTERMEYER

A POET'S PRAYER

God, though this life is but a wraith,
Although we know not what we use,
Although we grope, with little faith,
Give me the heart to fight—and lose.

Ever insurgent let me be;
Make me more daring than devout;
From sleek contentment keep me free,
And fill me with a buoyant doubt.

Open my eyes to visions girt
With beauty, and with wonder lit;
But let me always see the dirt
And all that spawn and die in it.

Open my ears to music;
Let me thrill with spring's first flutes and drums:
But never let me dare forget
The bitter ballads of the slums.

From compromise and things half done
Keep me, with stern and stubborn pride,
And when at last the fight is won,
God, keep me still unsatisfied.

ISAAC WATTS

O GOD, OUR HELP

O God, our help in ages past,
       Our hope for years to come,
Our shelter from the stormy blast,
       And our eternal home,

Before the hills in order stood,
       Or earth received her frame,
From everlasting You are are God,
       To endless years the same.

A thousand ages in Your sight
       Are like an evening gone,
Short as a the watch that ends the night
       Before the rising sun.

Time, like an ever-rolling stream,
       Bears all of us away:
We fly forgotten, as a dream
       Dies at the opening day.

O God, our help in ages past,
       Our hope for years to come,
Be now our guard while troubles last
       And our eternal home.

BIOGRAPHIES

By Emma R. Crossen
Harvard Divinity School

Akhnaton (14th century B.C.E), or Akhenaten, is credited with the first known attempt at monotheism. During his reign as king of Egypt, he tried to compel the nation to worship Aten (hence the name Akhen*aten*), a term used to designate the disc of the sun.

Alcuin of York (c. 735–804), had a long career as a teacher and scholar, first at the school at York and later as Charlemagne's leading advisor on ecclesiastical and educational affairs. From 796 until his death in 804 he was abbot of the monastery of St. Martin of Tours, which he developed into a model of excellence in education.

Lancelot Andrewes (1555–1626) was minister to both Queen Elizabeth I and King James I. During the latter's reign, Andrewes led the effort to translate the King James Version of the Christian bible.

Maya Angelou (1928–), hailed as a poet, educator, historian, best-selling author, actress, playwright, civil-rights activist, producer and director, continues to travel the world to international acclaim as a voice of wisdom.

Anselm of Canterbury (1033–1109) held the office of Archbishop of Canterbury from 1093 to 1109. He is called the founder of scholasticism, a movement which originally began to reconcile ancient classical philosophy with medieval Christian theology. Anselm is also famous for originating the ontological argument for the existence of God.

Waldemar Argow, Jr. (1916–1996) was ordained as a minister in June 1941 in Amherst, Massachusetts. He served Unitarian and Universalist congregations in Massachusetts and Philadelphia with his longest tenures in Cedar Rapids, Iowa and Toledo, Ohio. His father, Waldemar Argow, Sr., was a Unitarian minister in Baltimore, Maryland.

Aristophanes (c. 456–c. 386 B.C.E.) was a leading actor and writer in ancient Greek comedy. Only eleven of his forty plays survive, but these are the only complete plays that remain from Old Attic Comedy, a reference to the dramas of fifth-century Athens.

Augustine (354–430) is the best-known figure in the development of western Christianity. He is credited with framing the concept of just war. After starting his career as one of the best rhetoricians in the Latin world, Augustine converted to Christianity, gave up his career, and devoted himself to the priesthood. Even after being appointed Bishop of Hippo, he lived a monastic life. One of his many writings, *Confessions*, is a classic of world literature.

Marcus Aurelius Antoninus Augustus (121–180) was emperor of Rome from 161 to his death in 180. He is considered one of the most important Stoic philosophers. Antoninus' *Meditations*, which he wrote for his own self-improvement during military campaigns in Greece, is revered as a classic of literature, philosophy, and spirituality.

John Baillie (1886–1960) was a Scottish theologian and minister. During his career, he also served as President of the World Council of Churches and held university posts in the United Kingdom, United States, and Canada. His *A Diary of Private Prayer* is regarded as a devotional classic.

Karle Wilson Baker (1878–1960), a writer from Texas, became one of the most famous poets in the South through the publication of her poems in national journals like *Yale Review, Atlantic Monthly, and Harper's*. During the years 1914-1920, she was the most frequent contributor to the *Yale Review*.

Joseph Barth (1906–1988) was born in Salina, Kansas and went on to earn degrees from multiple universities before serving as minister at King's Chapel in Boston, Massachusetts. Beacon Press published his book entitled *The Art of Staying Sane*.

Monroe Beardsley (1915–1985), an American philosopher, was best known for his work in aesthetics. Beardsley promoted an instrumentalist theory of art. His published works include: *Practical Logic* (1950), *Aesthetics* (1958), and *Aesthetics: A Short History* (1966).

Ludwig van Beethoven (c. 1770–1827) was one of the most influential and famous musicians of all time. As a German composer and virtuoso pianist, he wrote, performed, and conducted orchestral and instrumental masterpieces, even after suffering total hearing loss in 1814. He was attracted to Enlightenment ideas and composed words and music to honor humanity.

Stephen Vincent Benét (1898–1943) was an American author, best known for his poems and short stories. In 1929, he won the Pulitzer Prize for *John Brown's Body*, a book-length narrative poem about the American Civil War.

William Blake (1757-1827) was an English mystic, poet, painter and printmaker, known for the philosophical and prophetic visions that informed his work. Although Blake objected to the established church, he had deep respect for religious experience, mythology, and scripture.

Anne Bradstreet (c.1612–1672), an immigrant from England to the Massachusetts Bay Colony, was the first woman to have her writings published in America. From a prominent Puritan family, both her father and husband served as governors of the colony. Bradstreet wrote on domestic and religious themes. Her poems document the difficulties of being a woman in Puritan New England. She was America's first published poet.

Marguerite Harmon Bro is the author of children's books, including the novel *Sarah*, first published in 1949.

Robert Burns (1759–1796) is widely regarded as the national poet of Scotland. Burns Night, a celebration of this beloved Scot, is practically a national holiday. The traditional Burns Night dinner usually begins with "Selkirk Grace" and concludes after the meal with singing of "Auld Lang Syne," which is also attributed to the poet.

Chief Yellow Lark was a Sioux Indian Chief in the late 19th century. He translated several Sioux prayers into English.

Max Coots (1927-) is Minister *Emeritus* at the Unitarian Universalist Church of Canton, New York, where he now creates whimsical ceramic sculpture.

J. Raymond Cope (1905–1988) served for 22 years as the pastor of First Unitarian Church in Berkeley, California, beginning in 1940. He previously taught philosophy at Indiana University. Cope was a community leader in Berkeley and participated nationally in the civil rights movement.

Samuel McChord Crothers (1857–1927) switched to the Unitarian Church in 1882 after beginning his pastoral career in the Presbyterian Church. In 1894 he became minister at First Parish in Cambridge (Unitarian) in Massachusetts. He was a popular preacher and distinguished essayist.

e. e. cummings (1894-1962) was a playwright, painter, and poet, known mostly as the latter. He was raised in a liberal family, his father a Harvard professor and Unitarian minister. He began writing poetry as a young child. Cummings' poems are marked by unconventional syntax, grammar, and punctuation. He received numerous honors, including a Guggenheim Fellowship, Bollingen Prize, and guest lectureship at Harvard.

Dadu (1544–1603) was a Hindu guru in Rajasthan, India. His group of followers became known as the Dadu-panth. Many of Dadu's words refer to natural joy and raising all earthly things to a divine status.

A. Powell Davies (1902–1957) rose to prominence as one of America's most forthright liberal spokesman from his position as pastor at All Souls Unitarian Church in Washington, DC from 1944 until his death. All Souls attendance grew to overflowing the church building, and seven new churches were established outside the city. He published several books on the Dead Sea Scrolls and *America's Real Religion*.

Dionysius of Alexandria (c. 190–265) became bishop of Alexandria in 248. Raised a pagan, he converted to Christianity after receiving a vision that he said persuaded him to study and refute the heresies of the church. Some of his more controversial positions included questioning the authorship of the Book of Revelation, and denouncing the Millenarian idea of Jesus Christ's return to earth. During his reign as bishop, Dionysius was forced into exile for years at a time during Roman persecution against Christians.

W.E.B. Du Bois (1868-1963) has been called the early-twentieth century's most prominent activist on behalf of African Americans. Upon his death, he had published 17 books and edited numerous journals. Du Bois also edited the NAACP journal *Crisis* (1910-1934) and promoted Pan-Africanism. He travelled to Ghana in 1961 and, after being denied a new U.S. passport, he and his wife became citizens of Ghana, where Du Bois died.

Elgin Cathedral was completed in the 13th century and is now a historic ruin in Moray, north-east Scotland. It was destroyed and rebuilt several times in three centuries. Following the Scottish Reformation in 1560, the building fell into decay until restoration efforts began in the 19th century.

Thomas Stearns (T.S.) Eliot (1888-1965), is one of the most widely-known poets of the twentieth-century. Born a member of a prominent Unitarian family in St. Louis, Eliot became a British citizen and joined the Anglican church around the age of 40. His poems, such as *Wasteland* and later works reveal a hope informed by his developing religious ideas. He received the Nobel Prize for Literature in 1948.

Epictetus (55-135) was a Stoic philosopher. Born a slave, he established a famous philosophical school in Nicopolis. Much of his work was transcribed by his pupil Arrian in *The Discourses* and *Enchiridion*. He encouraged living in accordance with reason and ways of nature.

Eleanor Farjeon (1881-1965), though best known for penning the hymn *Morning Has Broken*, wrote multiple volumes of poetry, satire, fiction, and drama for younger readers. She spent much of her life among the prestigious literary and theatrical circles of London. Her two novels about the character Martin Pippin are among her most famous.

Arthur Foote II (1911-1999) was a Unitarian Universalist minister at Unity Church in St. Paul, Minnesota from 1945-1970. He continued his family's tradition of creating new music for the church and also served in national leadership as the Chairman of the Hymnbook Commission of the Unitarian Universalist Association.

Harry Emerson Fosdick (1878-1969), a liberal Baptist minister in New York City, played a central role in the conflict between fundamentalism and liberalism in twentieth-century America. Amid controversy while serving a Presbyterian church, Fosdick was invited by John D. Rockefeller, Jr. to lead what became the interdenominational Riverside Church, where Fosdick was the first minister.

Francis of Assisi (c. 1181-1226) is perhaps the most popular saint for Catholics and persons of other faiths. Born the son of a wealthy businessman, he claimed to have experienced visions and spiritual crises in his twenties (following military service and medical illness) that inspired him to commit to a life of poverty and preaching among the people. He attracted a large group of followers who became the first order of Franciscan friars.

Stephen H. Fritchman (1902-1981), after starting his career in the Methodist Church, was ordained a Unitarian minister in 1930. While he was editor of the AUA journal, *The Christian Register*, Fritchman's editorial policies sparked an 18-month controversy in which opponents accused him of promoting communism and Soviet policies. He resigned in 1947 and went on to be minister of The First Unitarian Church of Los Angeles until his retirement in 1969. Under his leadership the church became a center of resistance to the Cold War, vigorously supporting liberal causes in the city and state.

Robert Frost (1874-1963) was a four-time Pulitzer Prize winning American poet of popular and frequently-quoted poems. He spent his adult life in New England, working as a teacher and a farmer. His first book of poems was published in England in 1913. He soon became a sought-after lecturer and poet. Some of his more famous works include "Birches," "The Road Not Taken" and "Stopping by Woods on a Snowy Evening."

Max Gaebler (1921-) was named one of the most influential citizens of the twentieth century in Madison, WI, where he served for 35 years as minister of the First Unitarian Society. During the turbulence of the 1960s, Gaebler was respected as a voice to facilitate inclusive debate on the University of Wisconsin campus. He served as interim minister in several international locations, including Japan, Canada, Australia, and the Vatican. These experiences encouraged Gaebler's concern and work for interfaith understanding.

Paul Gerhardt (1607-1676) was a German hymn writer, trained to be a Lutheran pastor during the religious conflicts of the 17th century in Germany. He is known as the "sweet singer of Lutheranism" and credited with writing more than 100 hymns and chorales. In the face of political pressure to repudiate certain Lutheran beliefs, he was unwilling to compromise even when it caused him to lose church employment.

Fred Gillis (1940-) is the Minister *Emeritus* of the Westminster Unitarian Church of East Greenwich, Rhode Island, which he served for twenty-six years. He was one of the original members of Abraxas, a community developing creative worship materials published as a Book of Hours for retreats.

Joan Goodwin (1926-2006) was an author and leader in liberal religious education. After working in religious education at Unitarian churches in Milwaukee and Cleveland, Goodwin worked at the Unitarian Universalist Association from 1973-1987. Her published works include *The Remarkable Mrs. Ripley: The Life of Sarah Alden Bradford.*

Edward Grubb (1854-1939) was a historian of Quaker thought and hymn writer. In addition to the hymn published here, Grubb also wrote *Quaker Thought and History: A Volume of Essays.*

Thich Nhat Hanh (1926-) is a Buddhist monk, writer, peace activist and acclaimed spiritual leader for followers of his mindful living practices. Hanh is credited with the concept of Engaged Buddhism, by which Buddhists apply insights from meditation to engage in social and political issues as part of their meditation and mindfulness practice. Martin Luther King, Jr. nominated Hanh for a Nobel Peace Prize in 1967.

Georgia Harkness (1891-1974) has been called one of the first significant American female theologians and the first woman professor at an American seminary. In addition to poetry, she published multiple books about such topics as Christian ethics and prayer. Harkness was integral in the movement to gain ordination for women in her own tradition, the Methodist church.

Donald S. Harrington (1914-2005) was a Unitarian minister at Community Church of New York and led New York's liberal party as state party chairman and candidate for lieutenant governor. Harrington used both political and church pulpits to speak liberal ideals.

John F. Hayward (1918-) a Unitarian minister, spent most of his career teaching and developing religious studies at universities. His tenure at First Parish in Columbus, Ohio ended sooner than he intended when the University of Chicago Divinity School offered him a faculty position to teach religion and the arts in 1951. Hayward finished his career at Southern Illinois University, where he was professor of philosophy, religion and the arts.

Gerald Heard (1889-1971) pioneered the consciousness-development movement known as Vedanta through writing, lecturing, disciplined meditation, and founding a small community for comparative-religious studies called Trabuco College in California. Heard came to the U.S. from England in 1937 to teach historical anthropology at Duke University. While in England, Heard was the BBC's first science commentator. He published more than thirty books.

Ralph N. Helverson (1912-2007) led First Parish in Harvard Square during the socially and politically turbulent decades from 1959 to 1977. Under his leadership, several initiatives developed and expanded, including media and social services. For many years, Helverson was the voice of Unitarian Universalism on Boston radio, where his distinctive Sunday morning broadcasts, *Window on Harvard Square*, brought the message of the liberal church to many people for the first time.

Frank O. Holmes (1898-1983) was ordained a Unitarian minister in 1921. He served parishes in Cambridge and Jamaica Plain, Massachusetts, and later in Concord, New Hampshire, and Oklahoma City, Oklahoma.

John Haynes Holmes (1879-1964) founded the Community Church of New York and helped to found the National Association for the Advancement of Colored People and the American Civil Liberties Union. He is remembered for his pacifism, preaching and writing celebrating the work of Mahatma Gandhi.

John Holmes (1904-1962) was a poet and professor of literature at Tufts University. While his own poetry was published in several volumes and frequently appeared in *The New Yorker*, Holmes' was also a pioneer in poetry education. He brought distinguished living poets to the Tufts campus long before poetry readings and poets-in-residence became a standard feature of academia.

Gerard Manley Hopkins (1844-1889) was a Jesuit priest and English poet. Most of his poetry remained unpublished until after his death, when he was recognized as one of the most daring Victorian poets for his innovative use of meter and imagery.

William de Witt Hyde (1858-1917) spent most of his career as president and philosophy professor at Bowdoin College in Brunsick, Maine. Hyde is credited with transforming the college into a model of higher education. Hyde's leadership and writings earned him a reputation as a theorist of higher education. His other published works include *God's Education of Man*.

James Weldon Johnson (1871-1938) was a leading figure in the Harlem Renaissance. Though best-known as a writer of novels, poetry, and folklore, Johnson was also an accomplished musician, professor, U.S. diplomat, anthropologist, and political activist. He wrote the lyrics to "Lift Ev'ry Voice and Sing," which has since been named the Negro National Anthem by the NAACP.

Daniel Ben Judah (c. 14th-century) was a poet of Jewish liturgy in 14th-century Rome. He composed the well-known hymn *Yigdal Elohim Hai* containing the thirteen articles of belief of Maimonides, one of the most prominent philosophers in Jewish history.

Kabir (1398 or 1448) was a mystic poet in India whose work remains in many sacred texts. His philosophy synthesized Hindu and Muslim concepts and promoted egalitarianism. He was one of the major inspirations to Sikhism.

Toyohiko Kagawa (1888-1960), Japanese pacifist and social reformer, became a Christian in his teens after taking a Bible class to learn English. He felt called to work among impoverished people and began by living in the slums of Kobe from 1910-1924. He organized unions and established hospitals, churches, and schools. He founded the Anti-War League and devoted his final years after World War II to reconciling democratic ideals with traditional Japanese culture.

Johannes Kepler (1571-1630) was a German mathemetician and astronomer whose observations about planetary motion changed astronomy and physics. He was motivated by a conviction that God created the world according to an intelligible plan and that this plan could be understood through reason. He developed the three laws of planetary motion and was the first astronomer openly to defend the views of Copernicus.

Sören Kierkegaard (1813-1855) was a prolific Danish Christian writer who contributed original concepts to theology, philosophy, literature, and psychology. He was especially critical of the state-church and its politics and formalities which, he said, distorted true Christianity.

D. H. Lawrence (1885-1930) was an English poet, novelist, and non-fiction writer. His most famous and famously controversial novel was *Lady Chatterly's Lover*. Lawrence's portrayal of sexuality and human instinct sparked controversy, opposition, censorship, and economic hardship for the author. His fiction is now recognized among the canon of great English novels.

Abraham Lincoln (1809-1865) was the U.S. president (1861-1865) during the Civil War which threatened to dissolve the nation. He is often credited with saving the union of states and ending slavery. Lincoln is the only U.S. president not to claim affiliation with a religious institution. He credited the Declaration of Independence as the text that most inspired him.

Samuel Longfellow (1819-1892) was a Unitarian minister and hymn writer whose sermons and lyrics reflected his transcendentalism. He served churches in Massachusetts, New York, and Pennsylvania and published four hymnals and a biography of his brother, the poet Henry Wadsworth Longfellow.

George MacRae (1928-1985) was an internationally known scholar of New Testament studies. He was ordained a Catholic priest in 1960 and went on to become the dean of Harvard Divinity School. MacRae served on the international committee that revised the Revised Standard Version of the Bible. He was the first Roman Catholic to be appointed director of the Society of Biblical Literature.

Peter Marshall (1902-1949) was a poor Scottish immigrant who came to the U.S at the age of 24 and became a famous Presbyterian minister and twice chaplain of the U.S. Senate. His wife, author Catherine Marshall, popularized Marshall's sermons and life story in several books, including *A Man Called Peter*, which was later made into an Oscar-winning film.

James Martineau (1805-1900) was an English Unitarian minister and educator whose widely influential theology and philosophy helped to shape 19th-century religious thought. His writings and sermons reflected his search for harmony between faith and reason and his emphasis on conscience as the ultimate authority for guiding human behavior.

Sidney Mead (1904-1999) was a historian of religion in the United States. He described the development of American Christianity as a tension between followers of reason and followers of revelation, and gives greater focus to the legacy of "rationalists." He was raised with American-Baptist affiliation and joined the Unitarian Universalist Association of Congregations while teaching at University of Chicago.

Edna St. Vincent Millay (1892-1950) a poet and playwright, was the first woman to receive, in 1923, the Pulitzer Prize for Poetry. The publication of her poem "Renascence" attracted the attention that earned her a scholarship to Vassar College, after which she moved to New York City where she wrote her famous volume, *The Harp-Weaver and Other Poems,* for which she won the Pulitzer.

Samuel H. Miller (1900-1968) was a Baptist minister and scholar who served as dean of Harvard Divinity School from 1959 until his death. His published works include *Man the Believer in an Age of Unbelief* (1968); his final work, *Religion in a Technical Age,* was published on the day of his death.

Mohammed (c. 570-632) is the founder of Islam, whose followers regard him as the last prophet in line with Adam, Noah, Abraham, and Jesus. The Islamic holy book, *Quran,* is the collection of revelations that Mohammed received when the prophet was in his forties.

Joachim Neander (1850-1680) was a German Reformed church teacher, theologian, and hymn writer. Many consider him the first important German hymnist after the Reformation.

Diann Neu is a feminist liturgist and psychotherapist and founder of WATER, the Women's Alliance for Theology, Ethics, and Ritual in Maryland. She has designed liturgies for international conferences and published articles and books on feminist approaches to ritual and liturgy.

Philipp Nicolai (1556-1608) was a German Lutheran pastor and poet who is best known as a hymn writer and musician. He is said to be the last of the Meistersinger tradition, in which one person composed both the text and melody. Nicolai's two most famous hymns were the inspiration for two cantatas by J.S. Bach.

Reinhold Niebuhr (1892-1971) is the best known American theologian of the 20th century. Niebuhr joined the faculty at Union Theological Seminary in New York City in 1928 after thirteen years as a pastor in Detroit, where he worked actively to counter the rise of the Ku Klux Klan in the burgeoning city. During World War II, he turned from pacifism toward his ideology of Christian Realism.

Ursula M. Niebuhr (1907-1997) founded the religion department at Barnard College in 1931 and continued as professor and chairwoman there for two decades. Born in Southampton, England, she was the first woman to win a fellowship to Union Theological Seminary. It was there she met the famous theologian, Reinhold Niebuhr, whom she married in 1931.

Else Niemoller is recognized as the wife and supporter of Pastor Martin Niemoller in his work against Nazi Germany. Though initially a supporter of Adolf Hitler, Pastor Niemoller later helped to found the Confessing Church and was imprisoned for 8 years in concentration camps for his opposition to state control of the churches. Else Niemoller died in a car crash in 1961.

John Oxenham (1852-1941) was the pseudonym for William Arthur Dunkerly, a prolific British poet, hymn-writer, and journalist. He used another pseudonym, Julian Ross, for journalism. In addition to hymns, he wrote more than 40 novels and books. Dunkerly was a deacon and teacher at Euling Congregational Church in London.

Theodore Parker (1818-1860) was a Unitarian preacher, lecturer, and public intellectual. Parker's calls for political, social, and economic reform earned him fame and dislike during his life. He led Boston opposition to the Fugitive Slave Act of 1850.

Francis Greenwood Peabody (1847-1936) left a legacy of lasting influences to Harvard University as professor (1881-1912) and dean (1901-1906) at the Divinity School. He introduced social ethics to the Divinity School curriculum and led the effort for Harvard to be the first traditional U.S. college to make daily religious service optional.

Leslie T. Pennington (1899-1974) came to Unitarian ministry from a Quaker background. During his 18 years in Chicago, he led church and community efforts that became national models of racial integration.

Folliott Sandford Pierpoint (1835-1917) was a British poet and hymnist. His most well-known composition is "For the Beauty of the Earth." Pierpoint taught classics and served as a schoolmaster in south-west England.

Plato (c. 428-348 B.C.E.), a student of Socrates and teacher to Aristotle, helped to lay the philosophical foundation for Western culture. He founded the first institution of higher learning in the Western world—the Academy in Athens.

Vivian T. Pomeroy (1883-1961) was a Congregational pastor and author of children's books. He was ordained in Bradford, Yorkshire, England. In 1923, he came to the United States where he served the First Congregational Parish (Unitarian) in Milton, Massachusetts for thirty years.

Ramanuja (c. 1020-1140) is revered by Hindus as a leading interpreter of the Vedanta school of Hindu philosophy. Ramanuja interpreted texts and developed a Vedantic philosophy known as Vaishnavism.

Walter Rauschenbusch (1861-1918) was a Baptist minister and leading theologian in the Social Gospel movement of the early twentieth century. He served congregations among impoverished workers in New York City and worked to improve social conditions and end child labor, inspiring leaders like Martin Luther King, Jr., and Mahatma Gandhi.

Martin Rinkart (1586-1649) was a German pastor and prolific hymn-writer during the Thirty-Years War. Rinkart was appointed Archdeacon at Eilenburg in 1917, just as the war began, and died shortly after it ended. Eventually, war, famine, and disease left him the only pastor in the city.

Wallace W. Robbins (1910-1988) was a Unitarian pastor and educator. He was president of Meadville Theological School at the University of Chicago from 1944-1956. After this appointment, he returned to his home state of Massachusetts to serve as minister of First Unitarian Church in Worcester.

Carl Sandburg (1878-1967), an American poet, won his first Pulitzer Prize in 1940 for a four-volume biography, *Abraham Lincoln: The War Years*, which followed *Abraham Lincoln: The Prairie Years*. His second Pulitzer came in 1951 for *Complete Poems*.

Lew Sarett (1888-1954) was a poet and professor. Audiences knew him as "poet of the wilderness" for his public lectures incorporating costumes and performance poetry to illustrate American Indian culture. At Northwestern University, he taught speech and English and co-authored widely used textbooks.

May Sarton (1912-1995) was an American poet, novelist, and memoirist. She published more than 50 books, including novels, plays, poetry, and memoirs. Sarton was known for probing the ordinary things of life to find deeper truths.

Sarum Primer is a collection of prayers and worship resources developed in Salisbury, England, during the 13th century. "Sarum" is the abbreviation for the Latin word for Salisbury. The collection was used throughout Britain, as well as parts of continental Europe, until the Reformation.

Dorothy L. Sayers (1893-1957), a British author, is best known for the popular mystery series featuring detective Lord Peter Wimsey. Sayers' Christian humanism and Anglican tradition are reflected in religious writings like *Mind of the Maker* and her translation of *The Song of Roland.* She revolutionized religious play-writing when she portrayed Jesus Christ speaking modern English in the television program *The Man Born to Be King,* which she wrote for the BBC children's hour. In her nearly ten-year advertising career, she developed popular campaigns for brands like Guiness and Colman's Mustard.

William Scarlett (1883-1973) was the bishop of the Episcopal Diocese of Missouri from 1933 to 1952. He is celebrated for his efforts to promote social reform after the Great Depression. Scarlett was also a close friend of theologian Reinhold Niebuhr.

Albert Schweitzer (1875-1965) was a theologian, writer, organist and physician. He won the 1952 Nobel Peace Prize for his philosophy of Reverence for Life. Schweitzer became a doctor in order to establish a missionary hospital in what is now Gabon, Africa, in 1914.

Seneca (c. 4 B.C.E-65 C.E.) was a Roman Stoic, government official, philosopher, and dramatist. His stoicism emphasized practical steps to confront life's dilemmas, especially mortality. His dramas continue to inspire writers today.

Vincent P. Silliman (1894-1979) was a Unitarian minister for 62 years. He edited *We Sing of Life.*

Socrates (470-399 B.C.E.) is credited with helping to establish the foundation for Western philosophy. He promoted critical reasoning and established the Socratic method of teaching, both of which employ critical questions in the pursuit of truth. Plato was Socrates' student.

Willard L. Sperry (1882-1954) was Dean of Harvard Divinity School and Minister of Harvard Memorial Church. Among his prolific publications are *Religion in America* and *Reality in Worship.*

Starhawk (1951-) is a pioneer in reviving earth-based spirituality and Goddess religion. She co-founded Reclaiming, an activist branch of modern Pagan religion, based in northern California. She is the author of *The Spiral Dance: A Rebirth of the Ancient Religion of the Great Goddess.*

Douglas Steere (1901-1995) was one of the leading Quakers of the twentieth century, a leading figure in the American Friends Service Committee and in the founding of Pendle Hill, a Quaker center outside Philadelphia. He was a professor of philosophy at Haverford College.

Jan Struther (1901-1953) was an English writer and hymnist. Struther created the character Mrs. Miniver in 1937 for a series of columns in *The Times* of London. The columns were first published in book form in 1939. MGM adapted the tales into the film Mrs. Miniver, the top film of 1942 in the U.S. and Britain..

Malcolm R. Sutherland (1917-2003) was a Unitarian minister, educator, and peace activist. At Meadville Lombard Theological School, he was professor, dean, and president from 1960-1975. Sutherland was recognized for promoting dialogue between religion and science.

Rabindranath Tagore (1861-1941), the 1913 Nobel Prize Laureate from Bengal, India, gained international fame through his poetry and tours in the early 1900s. Tagore supported Indian independence.

Teresa of Avila (1515-1582), was a Spanish Catholic mystic, writer and founder of monastic orders. She was canonized in the 17th century. In 1970, she became the first woman to be honored as a Doctor of the Church, a title designating the church's most significant writers.

Henry David Thoreau (1817-1862) was a writer best known for his book *Walden,* a reflection on two-years of simple living in natural surroundings, and the essay, *Civil Disobedience,* in which he defends individuals right to conscientious objecting in the face of unjust laws. His writings anticipated many elements of ecology.

Howard Thurman (1900-1981) was a minister, writer, and theologian. His most famous work, *Jesus and the Disinherited* (1949), inspired Martin Luther King, Jr. and laid a theological foundation for the civil rights movement. Thurman co-founded a racially integrated church in San Francisco. He was the first African-American dean of the chapel at Boston University.

Jacob Trapp (1899-1992) was a Unitarian Universalist minister who served congregations in Salt Lake City, Denver, and Summit, NJ. He was the editor of *Modern Religious Poems* and author of the hymn, "Wonders Still the World Shall Witness."

Tukaram (c. 1608-c. 1650) is a revered Indian poet and author of numerous texts. He was a devotee of Vitthal, a form of Lord Krishna. He was related to the Bhakti movement of the Maharashtra region of India.

Louis Untermeyer (1885-1977) was an author, poet, anthologist, and editor. He wrote or edited more than 100 books, including anthologies of short stories, humor, poetry, and children's literature.

Upanishads are part of the Vedas, the oldest sacred texts in Hinduism. The Upanishads are considered divinely inspired poetic liturgies, discussing meditation, the nature of reality, and philosophy. The texts vary in origin, dating from as far back as the seventh-century B.C.E. to the medieval or early modern period.

Herbert F. Vetter (1923-) is Minister at Large, *Emeritus*, of the First Parish in Cambridge, Unitarian Universalist, where he founded Cambridge Forum national radio and public television broadcasts and was a chaplain to Harvard University. He is the founder of Harvard Square Library.

Von Ogden Vogt (1879-1964) was minister at The First Unitarian Church of Chicago, adjoining the University of Chicago, from 1925-1944. He was celebrated as a master liturgist and visionary for the architecture of the church's grand Gothic structure, designed during his tenure. He wrote *Art and Religion* and *Cult and Culture* and coedited *Hymns of the Spirit and Services of Religion*.

Joachim Wach (1898-1955) was a pioneer scholar in the field of religious history. Born in Saxony, Wach was educated in Germany and later became a professor at University of Leipzig and University of Chicago.

Isaac Watts (1674-1748) is recognized as the father of English hymnody and a reknowned logician. He is credited with writing nearly 750 hymns, including "O God Our Help in Ages Past." He was pastor of a large independent church in London. His religious opinions were more ecumenical than most in his time.

Walt Whitman (1819-1892) is among the most influential and revolutionary poets and writers in American literature. Among his most well-known publications are *Leaves of Grass* (1855) and *O Captain! My Captain!* written to honor Abraham Lincoln after the president's assassination.

David Rhys Williams (1890-1970) was a Unitarian minister in Rochester, New York, from 1928 until his death. Williams was outspoken on social and political issues. Among his controversial opinions, he advocated racial toleration, birth control, labor organizing, and free speech.

Roger Williams (1603-1683) was a co-founder of the colony of Rhode Island. After coming to the United States in 1630, Williams advocated separation of church and state, fair treatment of Native Americans, and liberty of conscience.

End Note

If you discover any errors of omission or commission, please notify Rev. Herbert F. Vetter at www.harvardsquarelibrary.org or hfvetter@post.harvard.edu. Online corrections will be made immediately; print changes will be made as soon as possible in upcoming editions.

www.ingramcontent.com/pod-product-compliance
Lightning Source LLC
LaVergne TN
LVHW011353080426
835511LV00005B/276